...ducation,

...yment of leisure

SOCIETY, SCHOOLS,
AND PROGRESS IN JAPAN

SOCIETY, SCHOOLS, AND PROGRESS SERIES

General editor: Professor Edmund J. King

OTHER TITLES IN THE SERIES

For other titles of interest please see the end of this book.

The terms of our inspection copy service apply to all
the above books. Full details of all books listed and
specimen copies of journals listed will gladly be sent
upon request.

SOCIETY, SCHOOLS, AND PROGRESS IN JAPAN

BY

TETSUYA KOBAYASHI

PERGAMON PRESS
OXFORD · NEW YORK · TORONTO
SYDNEY · PARIS · FRANKFURT

U. K.	Pergamon Press Ltd., Headington Hill Hall, Oxford OX3 0BW, England
U. S. A.	Pergamon Press Inc., Maxwell House, Fairview Park, Elmsford, New York 10523, U.S.A.
CANADA	Pergamon of Canada, P.O. Box 9600, Don Mills M3C 2T9, Ontario, Canada
AUSTRALIA	Pergamon Press (Aust.) Pty. Ltd., 19a Boundary Street, Rushcutters Bay, N.S.W. 2011, Australia
FRANCE	Pergamon Press SARL, 24 rue des Ecoles, 75240 Paris, Cedex 05, France
WEST GERMANY	Pergamon Press GmbH, 6242 Kronberg-Taunus, Pferdstrasse 1, Frankfurt-am-Main, West Germany

Copyright © Tetsuya Kobayashi 1976

First edition 1976

Library of Congress Cataloging in Publication Data

Kobayashi, Tetsuya, 1926-
Society, schools, and progress in Japan.

(Pergamon international library of science, technology, engineering, and social studies): (Society, schools, and progress series)
Includes bibliographical references and index.
1. Education—Japan. I. Title.
LA1311.K62   1975   370′.952   75-33312
ISBN 0-08-019936-4
ISBN 0-08-019935-6 flexicover

Printed in Great Britain by A. Wheaton & Co., Exeter

Contents

Preface

This book has been prepared in an attempt to introduce the reader to some of the major features of national education in Japan. It consists of three parts. The first historical part, composed of the first two chapters, is designed to give the reader historical knowledge of Japanese education from early times to about 1950. The author believes it necessary to include such an historical section for a full understanding of the education of a country such as Japan, which has a long history and its own cultural tradition. The second part, the main body of the book, comprises five chapters, each of which is devoted to a certain aspect of the national education of contemporary Japan in the 1950s and 1960s. The final part, covering the early 1970s, intends to provide the reader with some idea of the prospects of Japanese education in the future. Throughout the whole book attempts have been made to give an analytical explanation of the relation between Japan's progress and its organized educational efforts, particularly in the schools.

It is, of course, too presumptuous to claim that in this small book all problems of Japanese education have been covered and treated in a balanced way, but the author hopes that the book, written by a Japanese, can offer some answers to the questions which non-Japanese readers might have had.

In writing the book, the author is indebted to many individuals among whom a few names should be mentioned for his special appreciation; Professor Edmund J. King, the general editor of the series, who offered the author a valuable opportunity to write this book; Dr. Benjamin C. Duke, who read and commented on part of the original draft; and Mrs. Anne Freifrau Grote, who corrected and typed the author's English manuscript.

The preparation for the book started and took place largely when the author was Director of the Unesco Institute for Education, Hamburg, and he would therefore like to dedicate the book to the UIE in memory of his pleasant association with the many friends who worked with him in the cause of Unesco.

Kyoto
Japan.

TETSUYA KOBAYASHI, PhD,
Professor of Comparative Education,
Kyoto University

Director, Unesco Institute
for Education, 1968–72

Note on Japanese names: in this book the names of the Japanese individuals, except for the name of the author which is expressed in the Western style, are written in the Japanese way, i.e. the family name first and the given name last.

CHAPTER 1

Historical Background I:
Japanese Education in the Pre-modern Period

EDUCATION IN THE FORMATIVE PERIOD OF THE NATION

Japan is made up of four main islands and several hundred smaller ones, and stretches in an arc, 1500 miles long from north to south off the coast of north-east Asia. This geographical position has had a significant effect on the character of the nation and its culture throughout its history. This was particularly true in its formative period. Because of its insularity, Japan is often compared to England, another island country on the opposite side of the Eurasian continent. It is interesting to note that both nations appeared in history in consequence of the impact of a superior culture from the continent.

In the case of Japan, this superior culture came from China, where by the third century BC its ancient culture had reached one of its peaks under the empire of the Sing and Hang dynasties. The encounter of the Chinese culture with the Japanese indigenous one was a slow process, extending over several centuries. One of the obvious reasons for this slowness is Japan's insularity. The Strait of Korea, the closest access to the continent, is 110 miles across, four times wider than the Straits of Dover. In ancient times, when the technique of navigation was primitive, it was wide enough to hinder any massive invasion, but allowed gradual influence from the continent. The impact of the Chinese civilization on the Japanese islands had thus become apparent by the fourth century AD.

The Chinese civilization brought into Japan superior weapons and tools which were not known hitherto in Japan, and which helped the transformation of the primitive society into a more superior one under a centralized power which had in its grasp the conveniences of a new civilization. By the fourth century Japan was already in the process of political unification in

1

which the ancestor of the present Imperial House attempted to make its hegemony over the local clans and to establish a centralized state which was eventually completed by the Taika Reform (AD 645).

Such a process was also assisted by other elements in the Chinese civilization, notably the writing system, the Chinese higher learning, and Buddhism. These elements provided the political rulers with the instruments of consolidating their rules. The first official record of the introduction of the literary culture into Japan was the visit of a Korean scholar in the Chinese classics to the Imperial House in 513. He was later succeeded by another Korean colleague who taught the Chinese classics at the Imperial House for some time. In 552 a Korean mission brought with them a Buddhist image and sutras. These events may be only a few examples of the greater flow of the Chinese civilization through Korea into Japan which should have been taking place since an earlier time. These elements of the Chinese civilization were accepted by the rulers in Japan as the symbol of their power as well as being a tool of government.

It was the Crown Prince Shotoku who for the first time attempted to form the government according to the Chinese pattern. While he was a youth he learnt about the Chinese classics and Buddhism from a Korean scholar in the Imperial House. During his office as regent (593—622) his efforts were devoted to setting up a government run by the bureaucracy in the place of the old loose federation of clans, and for this purpose he looked to China for guidance. In 603 an hierarchical system of twelve ranks was set up with the idea of appointing the officials by merit of service, an idea which sprang from Chinese political thought.

His adherence to Chinese learning appeared in his Constitution of Seventeen Articles, a set of injunctions issued in 604 which included quotations from various sources in Chinese classics. In 608 he sent a group of young students and priests away to study to the new ruler of the Sue Dynasty in China with the obvious intention of thus making the learning of the Chinese classics and the Buddhist scriptures the foundation of the new government. He himself devoted much of his time to scholarly pursuits, and named his newly built temple the Temple of Learning, implying his personal study as well as the place of his teaching. It is recorded that he often lectured on the sutras, while encouraging the youths of the court to learn from the Korean scholars attached to it.

His political success in setting up a consolidated government is questionable, but for our purpose it is enough to note that a great deal of educational activity took place in this politically formative period of the Japanese nation as a result of its contact with the literary culture of China. Such educational activities which were aimed at training youths in the new civilization took place informally without any formal system of education, such as was to be seen in the following period when the influence of the Chinese systems of government and education were more dominant.

The Taika Reform of 645 finally brought about a centralized government in Japan with the hegemony of the Imperial House over the traditional clans. The reform was led by Prince Nakano-Ohe, who later became Emperor Tenchi, and Nakatomino Kamatari. Both had studied under Minabuchi Shoan, who was among those sent to China by Prince Shotoku with a mission, and who had studied there for thirty-two years. Among the students who studied in China together with Minabuchi were Priest Min and Takamukono Kuromaro who on their return to Japan were appointed to the rank of "national doctor". Undoubtedly on their advice, the leaders of the Taika Reform attempted to build a centralized State on the model of contemporary China under the T'ang Dynasty. One of the things which they did immediately after the political takeover was to establish the legal system, which took over half a century to complete.

The Taiho Code of 701 was in fact the development of earlier codes which had been found to be incomplete because of their blind adoption of the Chinese law books. Although it was still Chinese in principle, the Taiho Code was readjusted to a reasonable extent for local needs. It consisted of twelve criminal codes and thirty administrative codes of regulations, the latter of which contained an Education Code, *gaku-rei.*

The Education Code was composed of twenty-two chapters which, according to the Chinese pattern, laid down the state system of education made up of a central grand school and provincial schools. The grand school, *daigaku-ryo,* was given two functions; on the one hand, it was a centre of moral indoctrination where Confucius was worshipped and where his doctrines on government and morals were disseminated among the government officials as well as the people. On the other hand, it was a school for potential bureaucrats whose qualifications were first of all the mastery of Confucian doctrines in government and morals.

Seven doctors and assistants taught from Confucian books of history and Confucian philosophy and laws as well as the basic reading and writing skills necessary for the mastery of Chinese literature. Four hundred students between the ages of 13 and 16 were to be selected from among the sons of the government officials. On passing the examination, students were to be recommended to the offices of the government.

In each province a provincial school was to be set up for the sons of the government officials and the influential men in the province. The number of the students varied according to the size of schools. From a "provincial doctor" the students received a similar but somewhat inferior education from those in the grand school.

The idea behind the Education Code was to supply government officials from among promising youths who were to be selected by their abilities and to be trained in the new knowledge and skills of government which had been introduced from the Chinese continent.

The idea of recruiting youths by ability was, however, to be limited by the reality of society. Thus the schools were open only to the sons of government officials and influential men in the provinces. Furthermore a loophole was provided for sons of the higher rank officials who were legally exempt from the examination for a government appointment. This was clearly a compromise made by the new government to meet the demand of the traditional families or clans who insisted on occupying posts in the government as their hereditary right.

Nevertheless, it is worth while noting that the first Japanese school system was set up with three distinctive characteristics which have since then been observed in most of the Japanese school systems through the ages, and which have, indeed, become almost inherent characteristics of Japanese schools. These three are the following: firstly, the schools were set up on the initiative of the government for the training of personnel necessary to the state, secondly, from an individual point of view, the schools provided a way to social success for ambitious youths, and thirdly, the schools taught the elements of a new civilization abroad, and thus functioned as an effective tool for allowing Japan to "borrow" a culture.

EDUCATION FOR THE ANCIENT ARISTOCRACY

The period of overwhelming sinonization of some three centuries was followed by one of readjustment during which the indigenous Japanese culture absorbed the implanted Chinese one and developed itself to a higher level. This period began roughly at the end of the ninth century with the discontinuation of the official missions to the Chinese Imperial Court. By this time the T'ang Dynasty was about to fail, and political unrest on the continent made official missions difficult and less attractive to the Japanese leaders.

The official disconnection with China did not mean a complete separation from the Chinese culture: trading ships continued to move between the continent and the Japanese islands, and priests and students in their private capacities visited China for study, but the elements of culture which they brought back were more limited in their sphere of influence, such as in the field of higher learning and in the style of life of the upper classes.

On the other hand, this official disconnection gave Japan the opportunity of integrating these foreign cultural elements with the indigenous ones, without it being overwhelmed by foreign influence, and thus Japan could develop the uniqueness of its individual culture to a higher level. This situation continued until the middle of the nineteenth century with one interruption in the sixteenth century when Japan's foreign relations policy tended once more towards being an active one.

A good example of the cultural adaptation was a system of writing. The Japanese language is totally unrelated to the Chinese, and, as mentioned earlier, no letters existed in Japan before the Chinese writing system was brought into Japan around the sixth century. While the ability to write Chinese in its classical form continued to be given a scholarly prestige until quite recently, Japanese had already begun in the seventh century to use certain of the Chinese ideographs in writing its tongue, not for their meaning, but for their sound value.

By the tenth century a Japanese system of writing had evolved in which Chinese ideographs were abbreviated and used for phonetic value. The innovation of this phonetic system, or *kana,* gave Japanese a freer way of expression and communication, a fact which accounted for the flourishing era of Japanese literature from the tenth to the twelfth century, but which certainly must have had a far-reaching effect on every aspect of the Japanese civilization.

Another example was the development of Buddhism, which was introduced to Japan also around the sixth century, and which had become a state religion under the patronage of the Imperial House by the eighth century.

During the course of development in the following next few centuries, the faith in Buddhism became stronger inside Japan by the evangelic efforts of Buddhist leaders who adjusted their doctrines and organizations to meet the religious needs of the Japanese people.

Nevertheless, Buddhism never superseded other systems of religion and belief, such as Shinto, an indigenous belief derived from the earlier primitive life of Japan, and Confucianism originating in China and brought to Japan together with other forms of Chinese civilization. Buddhism and other systems influenced each other in their doctrines and practices, but, nevertheless, remained side by side while retaining their own identities, thus creating a pattern of religious life which until now still prevails in Japan; Shinto for national and communal cults, Buddhism for meta-physical and spiritual questions, and Confucianism for secular morality and public ritual. This is, however, illustrating the matter in the simplest form and entailing a great risk of oversimplification.

The dominant social class in the early period of the development of the indigenous culture from the ninth to the twelfth century was that of the court aristocrats whose power had been inherited by their family lineage which descended from the ancient clan period. The higher posts in the government were given to those important members of the big families. Among them the Fujiwara family kept a special status by merit of its founder, Nakatomino Kamatari, and because of its matrimonial relation with the Imperial House, which eventually gave them an almost exclusive hereditary privilege in the head of the Fujiwara family being appointed regent.

These Fujiwara regents ran the government not so much through the government offices but more through their own household offices. At that time every big family had its household office for dealing with their family affairs, above all the management of its estates, which were the economic foundation of the family. As the centre of national government moved to the household office of the Fujiwaras, many of the government offices specified by the Taiho Code became nominal, and the roles of the officials in the Imperial Court became more ceremonial and social rather than political and administrative.

The last fact led to the creation of a peculiar culture of court aristocrats in whose social life aesthetic values played a dominant role. Men were judged not by their practical abilities nor by their ethical standards but by the aesthetic qualities of their taste and behaviour. Composing Japanese poems as well as Chinese ones, and playing a musical instrument were symbolically called the three essential skills for a man of nobility. Women, who shared such a cultural life with men, were expected to possess the same kinds of abilities.

Education in this period reflected the changing character of the culture of the time. With regard to the curriculum of the grand school in the national school system, a new emphasis on literary training had already been seen in the middle of the eighth century in the appointment of a doctor of literature to the school. By the beginning of the ninth century the literature course had become so popular that the course had to be limited only to those students from the highest ranks of the aristocratic families.

By the tenth century a decline of the grand school had been recorded. The sons of the higher ranks of aristocratic families were less eager to enter the school. The qualities of students as a whole declined. The school found it difficult to maintain the building because of the lack of government support.

The reasons for such signs of decline were obvious. The sons of the higher ranks of aristocratic families were exempted by the School Code from the examination for government posts. Even the appointments to the minor posts were too often made not on the individual's abilities but because of his family. When the government posts became nominal, who should then care about training for such posts in the grand school? Thus when its buildings were destroyed by fire in 1177 no reconstruction was done and the school ceased to exist.

The situation of provincial schools was similar but worse. The plan in the Taiho Code must have been too ambitious, and, according to the records, only a few schools actually existed. The school in northern Kyushu was said to enjoy a high standard of teaching at one time, being situated at the gateway to continental China, but by the tenth century there was no trace of it in existing records.

In contrast to the decline of the state system, the prosperity of the private schools in this period was noteworthy. These private schools originated in the boarding houses built by the big families for the sons of some branch of the families in the provinces who came up to the capital to attend the grand school. As the grand school failed to guarantee government posts for the ambitious youths, the big families converted the boarding houses into their own schools, where the youths of a family received the education necessary for a government post or to manage the family estates. Thus from the eighth to the thirteenth centuries at least five private schools existed according to the records.

EDUCATION FOR THE WARRIORS

By the end of the twelfth century a new social class superseded the court aristocrat and established the military government. These military people originated from the estate keepers of the aristocratic families in the provinces. At a time when there was no local police system, they armed themselves and ruled by might of arms. Finally, taking advantage of the instability of the central government, they took over political power from the hands of the court aristocrats and established the military government which lasted under six successive military families for seven centuries from the end of the twelfth century to the later part of the nineteenth.

Under this military government special kinds of educational activity took place. There were differences, however, in nature and form between the education of the early period of the military dominance and that of the later period under the Tokugawas. Therefore, mention will first be made of the educational activities of the early period from the thirteenth to the sixteenth centuries.

The military class who thus emerged possessed a culture different from that of the court aristocrat. It was essentially a non-literary culture. Literary abilities were regarded as less important, although excellence in both literary and military arts was often regarded as the ideal cultural refinement. With a few distinct exceptions who have been known as warrior-scholars or artists, the majority of the ranks of the military class were illiterate. Indeed, it was only after the seventeenth century that the military class transferred themselves to the military-bureaucratic class and literary abilities were required to carry out this new function. Until then, military men were essentially fighting men, and for them abilities in the fighting skills were most important.

This did not mean that they lacked any culture, however. On the contrary, they created a type of culture in which the behaviour of men was judged by their moral standards. The word *bushido* or chivalry appeared at a later time, but the moral qualities implied in *bushido,* such as courage, bravery, perseverance, fidelity, and loyalty, already regulated the way of life of the warriors of the period. It was not through reading books, but through experience of life in the family and community and above all in battle that such qualities were acquired.

The man responsible for the training of youths was the head of the family. A number of existing family precepts written during the period between the thirteenth and the fifteenth century indicate what kind of training was undertaken at that time, but there must certainly be more unwritten family creeds which had an educational function for the younger members of warrior families.

Living in such a non-literary culture it was natural that the military class till the seventeenth century never established its own school system except for a few isolated efforts of setting up schools or libraries. As mentioned earlier, the organized educational activities of the court aristocrats in the state school system and private schools had discontinued by the end of the twelfth century. It was now the Buddhist temples that filled the gaps in institutionalized education in the period between the thirteenth and sixteenth centuries.

From the beginning of their establishment, the Buddhist temples had an educational function of training the priests in reading the sutras, which required certain literary knowledge. As time went on, the training of priests in various Buddhist sects became more systematic and was broadened and included secular literary studies both at a basic and at higher levels with a consequent appearance of many literary figures among the priests after the eighth century.

By the twelfth century, when other educational institutions ceased to exist, the Buddhist temples and monasteries remained under the patronage of the military governments as centres of education and higher learning by producing priest scholars, and at the same time by starting to take lay children for their elementary education. The highest peak of scholarly activity in the Buddhist temples was in the fourteenth and fifteenth centuries, when the major temples of *zen* sects received a high scholarly reputation in Chinese literature. This continued until the seventeenth century when the Buddhist temples discontinued secular scholarly activities, leaving this function in the hands of lay schools which once more emerged under the new auspices of the Tokugawa military government.

The practice of educating lay children in the Buddhist temples began around the thirteenth century. Because of the Buddhist egalitarianism the temple accepted children from all social classes. By the fifteenth century it had become a somewhat common practice among wealthy commoners to send their children to the temples for a few years' elementary education alongside children of the military class.

The appearance of the commoners in the history of education indicates the socio-economic changes in Japanese society in the fifteenth and sixteenth centuries, during which Japan engaged in economic activity and saw the rise of the merchant class in the towns. One of the sources of their wealth was the overseas trade which first took place in the thirteenth century, first with China and then by the sixteenth century extending to the South Seas and further to the Western world. Trade with the latter was carried out by adventurous Portuguese and Spaniards, through whom Japan for the first time discovered the West.

The effect of these contacts was not limited to the economic life of Japan. The Japanese culture which had been taking its own course of development after the official disconnection with China at the end of the ninth century now received new stimulation for further progress from China, the South Seas, and the Occidental world. The renewed contact with China resulted in the flourishing of the study of Chinese literature notably in *zen* temples in the fourteenth and fifteenth centuries.

With regard to the impact from the West, Christianity and guns respectively represented the spiritual and material elements of the Occidental civilization brought into Japan. Christianity did not last long, however, and its influence upon the spiritual and cultural life of the Japanese remained local. In the field of education, the Spanish missionaries established a few church schools and seminaries which were only short-lived. The guns, on the other hand, changed the art of war and resulted in the emergence of a centralized military power of the Tokugawas which, armed with these supreme weapons, finally brought to the nation a political stability in the seventeenth century after a long period of political and military struggle.

TOKUGAWA EDUCATION

One of the distinguishing features of Tokugawa education was its conservatism, in which respect, of course, it reflected Tokugawa society itself. When the first Tokugawa Shogun Ieyasu set up his *bakufu* (or warrior government) in Edo (now Tokyo) in 1603, the prime objective of the regime was to establish political stability in the country. Ieyasu and his successors worked out an elaborate socio-political system which, on the one hand, kept the country at peace for more than 200 years but, on the other, hindered all efforts at social change or progress. Society was rigidly stratified into classes, each to be content with its legally defined status and obligations. Law enforcement machinery was provided both by the central *bakufu* and by the local *han* (feudal domains or baronies). Communication with the outside world was strictly prohibited by the government's policy of seclusion.

Education was from the beginning regarded as a most effective tool for conserving the *status quo* and was encouraged by Ieyasu and his successors. The aim of education was to fit the people into the existing social and political order. The conservatism of Tokugawa education was manifested in the unquestioned authority of teachers over students and in the dogmatic character of its instruction. As official doctrine, the *bakufu*, adopted the Chu Hsi School of Confucianism, which prescribed the orderly interrelationship of cosmos and human society. The regime prohibited Western learning, not only because of its association with Christianity but also because of its novelty.

Nevertheless, by encouraging education, intellectual ferment spread, and new schools of thought gradually developed. Toward the end of the Tokugawa era, heterodox schools of Confucianism such as Wang Yang-min (Yohmei-ha in Japanese), and the so-called "national learning" or *kokugaku* (the study of Japanese classics) developed strongly. Even "Western learning" came in for greater study. So long as the Tokugawa government remained firm, the heterodox scholars were kept under control or even utilized to reinforce the regime. But when the regime lost its unchallenged position, the heterodox scholars became the driving force for the political reforms that led to the Meiji Restoration of 1868.

Tokugawa society was characterized by a strict stratification of classes and a highly restricted social mobility. Status was determined by birth. *Samurai* (warriors) had become a hereditary administrative class. The aim of education was to prepare people to behave and function in accordance with their hereditary status. Therefore it was organized on a class basis. The main distinction was between education for *samurai* and education for the commoners. The former provided the élite with the qualities deemed necessary for rulers; the latter aimed to mould the masses into efficient and obedient followers.

Paradoxically, however, the concept of education for social mobility was not completely alien to Tokugawa society. Education was, in fact, a means of social mobility − limited, but still significant − for a small number of people, particularly for commoners, who might move to *samurai* status by becoming professional scholars, priests, or doctors. These professions were open to talent, without regard for origin, and thus ambitious youth of lowly origin sometimes managed to enter the professions and, by dint of hard work, achieve "simulated" or even full *samurai* rank.

In the latter part of the Tokugawa period, the official educational system was used more deliberately to search out "people of talent". The new pressures from the outside world, coupled with internal economic problems, made the shortage of able leaders clear, and increasingly talented people were recruited from the lower *samurai* class. This was a risky game, and it could work only in so far as these upstarts remained loyal to the regime. When, later, they turned their backs on the *status quo,* the Tokugawa government was replaced by the Imperial Meiji government, which succeeded in attracting these new elements.

Throughout the Tokugawa period there was no central office of education. This was in contrast to the ancient period when the *daigaku* functioned as a central educational ministry, and to the modern period, when the strong Ministry of Education is central to the large educational bureaucracy. The Shoheiko, or Tokugawa school of higher learning, existed throughout most of the period as a centre of learning and education, but the head of the Shoheiko functioned only as head of this school and as Confucian ritual master to the government. He had no control over the schools of the *han* governments.

Nevertheless, there was a high degree of uniformity in educational practice. This was due partly to the fact that the Tokugawa society was, despite its feudalistic appearance, fairly centralized and uniform in administration. In the cultural sphere as well, there was a fair degree of homogeneity. Kyoto and Osaka first led, and then, by the latter part of the Tokugawa period, Edo came to dominate the cultural life of the country. The Shoheiko did, in fact, play an important role in the unification of education. As the official school of *bakufu*, the Shoheiko's influence extended over *han* schools in organization and teaching. Its graduates occupied at one time more than a third of the total number of *han* school teaching positions.

Commoners' schools were also not centrally regulated, yet there was a fairly high uniformity in organization and teaching. Many of the teachers were directly or indirectly under the influence of education and cultural centres in Edo, Kyoto, or Osaka.

Education was fairly well spread over the country. It is not easy to estimate the quality and level of literacy of the period, but it is quite clear that *samurai* were highly literate. This may be seen in their school curricula, the qualifications required of them by the bureaucracy, and their literary life. For the commoners, it is generally agreed that about 40 to 50 per cent of the male population and about 15 per cent of the female population were literate or had received formal education.

Tokugawa education was entirely secular. In the first place it was completely under the control of either secular government or of private individuals. Although many Buddhist priests taught in private schools for commoners, the Buddhist sects as such had no specific educational policies. The priests taught in their private capacities.

Secondly, the content of Tokugawa education was never religious. The Buddhist sacred books seem rarely, if ever, to have been used in the common schools. Textbooks were either Confucian or secular. Confucianism could function as a religion, but in the field of education it functioned as a completely secular instruction in literature, ethics, and history or political science in the present sense of these words. Thus Japan did not experience the conflict of State and Church that marked the history of European education.

The Warriors' Schools

There were three types of institutions for *samurai* education: *bakufu* schools, *han* schools, and private schools. They were entirely for boys; girls were usually educated informally at home.

Throughout its reign, the Tokugawa government provided directly under its control twenty-one *bakufu* schools, each different in educational function. The most important was the Shoheiko, or Shoheizaka-gakumonjo, the highest institution of Confucian learning of the time. The school was founded originally by Hayashi Razan in 1630 with government help, and run by the Hayashi family. In 1691 the Hayashi family officially granted the authority to direct ritual ceremony as well as learning in the school, and the Shoheiko was to be run under the auspices of the Tokugawa government.

Only *samurai* were allowed to attend, but sons of the commoners who intended to devote their lives to scholarly work were allowed to put their names at the end of the enrolment book. The courses were divided into three parts: Confucian literature, history, and composition. Teaching was carried out by lecturers, seminars, and individual tutoring. In 1790 the government forbade teaching the doctrines of schools other than the Chu Hsi school in this institution. After that, Shoheiko became a centre of the official Chu Hsi doctrine.

Other important *bakufu* schools were established mostly in the latter part of the Tokugawa period: Igakukan or School of Oriental Medicine (established in 1795); Wagaku-kodansho or School of Japanese literature (1793); Bansho-torishirabejo or School of Occidental Literature (1856); Kobujo or School of Occidental Military Science (1856); Gunkan-sorenjo or Navy School (1857); and Igakusho or School of Occidental Medicine (1858). All continued in existence until the end of the Tokugawa regime, and some of them were transformed into modern educational institutions of the new government.

Except for the land directly governed by the central *bakufu,* the country was divided into some 300 large and small *han,* or feudal domains, each independently governed but under the suzerainty of the central government. Most *han,* at least towards the end of the Tokugawa period, had one or more *han* schools which were commonly called *hanko, hangaku,* or *hangakko.* They were established for *samurai* boys, but some *hanko,* especially in the latter Tokugawa period, admitted sons of upper commoners.

In the early period, *han* schools followed the pattern of the Shoheiko, and the emphasis was laid on Confucian teaching. In the eighteenth century they began to include in their curricula such practical subjects as applied mathematics, military science, medicine, and astronomy. Although all of these schools were later abolished by the new Meiji government, local pride has kept their names alive in some areas by using them for the local high schools.

Besides these government schools, there were many *shijuku,* or private schools, for *samurai.* Some of them were supported by local governments, morally or materially, while others were completely independent. Typically, they specialized in particular curricula: Confucian learning, Japanese studies, Western languages, medicine, mathematics, military science, and so on. Their status depended upon the reputation of their teachers for scholarship. Some with nationwide reputation were attended by students from throughout the country, while others were attended only by local students and were small in size. For *samurai* children it was common to attend first a *shijuku* and then a *han* school, or attend them simultaneously.

Samurai education was often regarded as a cultural and social symbol of higher social status. During 270 years of internal peace under the Tokugaea, the *samurai* class had been transformed in character. They were no longer a military class in a strict sense, although the military outlook was never entirely forgotten as a discipline and as a symbol. Instead, they had become a leisure class engaged primarily in routine bureaucratic work.

The founder of the Tokugawa House, Ieyasu, had encouraged "literary learning on the left hand, military arts on the right hand" in his Law of Military Houses. By this he proposed that their crude military character should be tempered by cultural refinements, and that their leisure time should be occupied with military as well as literary training. Ieyasu's policy was loyally followed by his successors and the *han* lords. This view was vigorously propagated by such ideologies of *bushido* (or the way of *samurai*) as Yamaga Soko, Kumazawa Banzan, and Ogyu Sorai.

In time of war, the *samurai* class could distinguish itself from the rest of the population by their military leadership. But in peacetime some other mode of distinction had to be sought. Education came to serve this purpose: it was the character of education available that distinguished *samurai* from the common people. The content of education reserved for *samurai* served to symbolize their status. Such subjects as the Confucian classics, which were taught at the *samurai* schools, were important not only because of the content but also because it could be sported as a status symbol. It was taught only to *samurai* or to upper commoners who might be allowed to identify with them.

This should not suggest, however, that *samurai* education had only cultural and symbolic functions. It had also a practical function. Government was still simple enough so that the wisdom of the sages taught in the Confucian classics had practical meaning. When leadership depended primarily upon the moral quality of individuals, the study of Confucianism was, through its moral instruction, a practical preparation for the work of administration. Routine clerical and administrative work was in the hands of the lower-rank *samurai,* who needed not only moral training but some practical training as well. In Matsumoto *han,* for example, mathematics was taught only to the lower *samurai.*

Since the *bakufu* and *han* schools were under strict government control, there was no academic freedom in the sense this is meant in European universities. Education supported the *status quo* and promulgated orthodoxy; there was no free search for truth for its own sake. The prohibition of unorthodoxy at the Shoheiko in 1790 was an example of the control in the government schools. But the private schools were also not immune.

In 1839 a group of the "barbarian school" (scholars in Western studies) were imprisoned for unorthodoxy. Nevertheless, the private schools had relatively more freedom, and therefore it is not difficult to understand that such scholars as Tominaga Nagamoto, Hoashi Banri, and Ando Shoeki, whose theories were far in advance of the times, had neither studied nor taught in the government schools. By the same token it was natural that the anti-feudal *kokugaku,* or Japanese (as distinct from the Confucian or Chinese) studies, also prospered outside the government schools.

Samurai education was based primarily on the classical Confucian tradition, comparable in some ways to the humanistic tradition of medieval European universities. When the realists tried to reform European universities by introducing practical subjects, there was much conflict. In Japan a similar, but much diminished, development occurred. Practical subjects, such as mathematics, medicine, and other Oriental style sciences, were traditionally excluded from the *samurai* curriculum except for lower-ranking *samurai* or the scholarly and medical professions. When the study of the practical Western sciences became necessary it was the lower-ranking *samurai* and scholars or doctors who were most willing to learn.

Western learning was, however, acceptable only in the applied sciences. Philosophy and the social sciences remained formally unorthodox. People stimulated to critical unorthodoxy by Western studies were suppressed, as in the "barbarian school" case. Because free inquiry was severely restricted, science in the modern sense never developed systematically in the *samurai* schools. The classical tradition overshadowed realism despite the introduction of some practical elements to the *samurai* curriculum.

The concept of searching out talent through education was development of the later Tokugawa period. It arose in response to the practical needs of the central *bakufu* as well as the local *han* governments, facing inner crisis, to rely on their human resources for reconstruction. Therefore it is expected to see that the periods of rapid development of *bakufu* and *han* schools coincided with those of crisis and reconstruction. Particularly after the beginning of the nineteenth century, many *han* schools were newly built or else reorganized with the specific object of searching out talent in relation to the *han* reform programme.

Education for the Commoners

For commoners, the most important educational institution was *terakoya*. The word *terakoya* originated in the previous period when children of all classes received their elementary education in *teru* (or temples). They were called *terako* or children of the temple. In the Tokugawa period the educational function of the temples was shared by other agencies as the demand for education increased among the commoners. In addition to Buddhist temples, Shinto shrines and private houses were utilized for popular education, where literate commoners, Shinto and Buddhist priests, and *ronin,* or *samurai* without feudal ties, taught children. Despite their religious origin, *terakoya* in the Tokugawa period had lost all religious functions and had become entirely secular.

Terakoya was a completely voluntary organization, unregulated by government. There were variations in organization, curriculum, and courses of study, but they fell into a general pattern. The number of children in a *terakoya* ranged in general between twenty and fifty. But in the large cities, such as Edo and Osaka, some had more than 100 children, and at least five were attended by more than 300. Usually there was a single teacher, who was occasionally helped by his wife, son, or older children. In such cases the teacher was also the manager of the *terakoya.* But sometimes teachers were hired by local individuals or groups. In the latter case the situation was more similar to the present school organization.

Unlike *samurai* schools, *terakoya* accepted both boys and girls. Usually the child first entered *terakoya* at the age of 6 or 7 and continued his or her education until 10 to 13, from which ages apprenticeship began. Teaching was based on individual tutoring concentrating on reading, writing, and calculation, with the addition of sewing for girls. Reading and writing, however, went beyond mere rudimentary levels. In the process of learning these skills, children studied what are now called social studies, vocational arts, and moral values, which provided them with the knowledge and skills they needed for future jobs and more immediately for apprenticeship.

Reliable statistics on *terakoya* are lacking, but one source shows that toward the end of the Tokugawa period there were some 1200 *terakoya* in and around Edo and that the total number in the country was about 15,500. They were found mainly in towns, but a not inconsiderable number were found in villages, attended mainly by the upper strata of the villages.

Terakoya influenced the lives of the commoners so much, particularly after the middle of the Tokugawa period, that the governments, both *bakufu* and *han*, began to pay attention to them. In some cases they were encouraged (and also checked upon) by grants of a popular Confucian morals text or by awards of prizes to meritorious teachers. Generally, however, the government did not aim at direct control. When they decided that popular education required control, they set up a different type of institution, *gogaku*, or village school, which was also called *kyoyujo*, or hall of precepts.

Gogaku was, unlike *terakoya*, a gracious "benevolence" to the commoners. In the Confucian conception the rulers had the obligation of teaching the proper way of life to the ruled, their moral and mental inferiors. *Gogaku* also had a more calculating purpose of countering political and economic unrest which was growing among the commoners. The *gogaku* curriculum was based on Confucial doctrines with emphasis on moral indoctrination for the obedient industrious workers. The number of *gogaku* is not accurately known, but a document shows that at one time at least some 130 existed throughout the country.

Under-girding this fairly developed system of commoner education was the economic progress of Tokugawa Japan. During this period commerce had expanded beyond the narrow limits of local communities, and for the merchants some literary knowledge, together with some calculation skill, was essential. Although training in an occupation was acquired through apprenticeship, some knowledge and skills were prerequisite. There was less need for literacy on the part of farmers. Nevertheless, upper-class farmers came increasingly to need it as their contacts with merchants expanded and as some of them started to operate small industries. The general rise in the economic level also made it possible for the commoners to maintain their own schools. Most *terakoya* were supported by fees, while some were maintained by private donations. It was increasingly recognized by the people themselves that the sacrifice of money and time for education was economically worth while.

Popular culture in the Tokugawa period also reached a level where literacy became necessary in order to enjoy it. And the existence of large numbers of literate readers in turn stimulated the wider circulation of popular literature. The consumers were mostly townspeople who had the time and money to afford such leisure pursuits. In the villages the ordinary peasants had neither the time nor the money, and only the upper-class farmers could enjoy it. Commoners did not limit themselves merely to popular literature. *Kokugaku* (Japanese studies) found its most enthusiastic supporters among the wealthy townspeople as well as the upper farming class in the villages. Some also showed considerable interest in Confucian studies.

Some commoners also required literacy because of their social and administrative responsibilities. Upper-class commoners were often appointed as *machi-yakunin* (town officers) or *mura-yakunin* (village officers). They occupied the lowest position in the bureaucratic hierarchy, but the highest position in the towns and villages. It was they who passed government regulations and announcements downward to the common people, and reports, petitions, and requests upward to the government on behalf of the town and village poeple. Therefore they required literacy of a comparatively high level. Furthermore, because of their position in the bureaucratic hierarchy, they often identified themselves with the *samurai* rulers and, accordingly, became interested in Confucian studies, the status symbol of *samurai.* They attended *shijuku,* and in some limited cases even *han* schools for Confucian studies.

The development of popular education, regardless of its original intention, awakened the popular consciousness. The general rise of cultural standards in this period is often attributed to education. But education also went on to create some class consciousness among the commoners. Education, together with other social developments, gave the people some ideas on individual qualities which were apart from hereditary determinants such as family or class. Although this was still far from individualism in the modern sense, nevertheless the people became concerned more with individuals than with family status or class, and the attitude of the commoners towards the ruling class began to change. Increasingly, wealthy townspeople became independent of their lords, and even ordinary peasants showed signs of self-assertion, as may be seen in the growing number of peasant upheavals during the latter Tokugawa period.

Nevertheless, the relationship between ruler and ruled was, generally speaking, less antagonistic. Education was at least partly responsible. As mentioned earlier, Tokugawa society, despite its general rigidity, allowed social mobility though on a limited scale. In fact, there were a few channels of upward mobility from upper commoner to *samurai* status of which education was the most important. Therefore, ambitious youth of the commoner class, who might otherwise have become a discontented element in society, was elevated to the *samurai* status or its equivalent by his education, and thereby lost his class antagonism toward the ruling *samurai*.

Another reason the popular awakening did not necessarily result in class hatred has to do with the quality of the education. Popular education, particularly in *gogaku*, was infused with a Confucian moralism from which no criticism of the class system could come. *Terakoya* was more concerned with the practical aspects of the commoners' life, but its teaching was also under the moral influence of the age. Furthermore, its training was too vocationally orientated to develop critical minds.

Ferment for National Education

Throughout the Tokugawa period the question of education had been fairly extensively discussed by scholars and scholar-administrators. Towards the end of the eighteenth century they touched upon the problems of a system of national education, and at the same time some programmes developed in the direction of national education. As we shall see later, the plan for national education of the following Meiji government was very Western in character — quite alien to Tokugawa education. Nevertheless, the Meiji plan could not have been so easily adopted if the idea of national education had been completely foreign and if there had been no such experiment before it was adopted.

One of the early discussions was made by Nakarai Chikusan, a Chu Hsi scholar in Osaka. He submitted to *bakufu* some advisory notes, *Sobo Kigen,* between 1789 and 1791, in which he developed his concept of national education. He recommended that higher institutions be set up in the large cities of Edo, Osaka, and Kyoto, to which the talented of the society should be sent regardless of social origin. *Terakoya,* he proposed, should be transformed into public institutions so that each town and village would have elementary schools.

Toward the end of the Tokugawa period, arguments on national education took place more frequently. Hoashi Banri proposed to set up an academy of military arts and Confucian learning in Edo, and a school of Confucian, *kokugaku,* and Occidental learning in Kyoto. He also suggested the transformation of all Buddhist temples into elementary schools. Hirose Tanso, a Confucian scholar, urged the necessity of searching for talent through the schools, and compulsory attendance for all children, whatever their classes.

Sato Nobuhiro, an Occidental scholar, developed an ambitious plan. A Ministry of Education and Morals should be established in the capital with the function of controlling all schools in the country. In areas with a certain population there should be ten elementary schools for the children over the age of 8. In larger communities, an additional school should be set up where advanced subjects should be taught to the most talented. After the age of 15 the ablest would move to a national academy. He even proposed kindergartens for pre-school children. Oka Kumaomi, a disciple of the Hirata school of Japanese classics, made a strongly nationalistic argument: universal education would implant nationalistic ideology in the people's minds.

Later, *bakufu* and some *han* governments set up programmes inspired by the concept of national education. It was short-lived and transitional. The reform movement in *bakufu* was a result of the recommendation by Hayashi Akira, head of the Shoheiko, in 1858 that elementary schools be established in various places. In 1862 *bakufu* appointed two eminent

Confucian scholars, Yoshino Kinryo and Yasui Sokken, as *gakumonjo-bugyo,* or the Secretaries of Education. Because of political crises, these posts were abolished after three years, but during this short period of existence they made some attempts to modernize the educational system.

In 1863 *bakufu* ordered the establishment of elementary schools in Edo. In the same year the *bakufu* School for Occidental Studies was reorganized, becoming literally a school of Western studies rather than simply a school of foreign languages. The curriculum included astronomy, geography, philosophy, mathematics, chemistry, physics, mechanics, drawing, and painting, as well as foreign languages such as Dutch, English, French, German, and Russian. Even the centre of Confucian conservatism, Shoheiko, was forced to reform. In 1865 Hayashi Akira, its head, emphasized the teaching of practical subjects, and in 1867 the introduction of administration, foreign studies, and Japanese history was planned for this pre-eminently Confucian centre.

Local experiments were conducted by some *han* governments mostly during the short period prior to the abolition of the *han* system in 1871. In 1868 Shizuoka *han* adopted a universal elementary school system. Its Numazu Military Academy Elementary School was known as one of the successful experiments of the time. Kyoto established sixty-four elementary schools in 1869, which were praised at the time as a good example of a school system based on local school districts.

Fukuyama *han* was one of the most progressive. The 1867 reform opened the doors of the *han* schools to commoners. In 1870 the *han* government published a reform plan providing for general education in common schools and professional training in higher schools. Girls' schools were also to be established. In 1871 *keimojo,* or institutes for popular enlightenment, were set up as centres of elementary and adult education. Iwakuni *han* was another example of educational reform. In 1871 it established a system of elementary, secondary, and foreign language schools aiming for universal education. The reform of Saga *han* combined a *han* school with *terakoya* in order to make the new system universal.

CHAPTER 2

Historical Background II:
Japanese Education in the Modern Period

ESTABLISHMENT OF THE NATIONAL SYSTEM OF EDUCATION

In 1867 the Meiji emperor wrested sovereignty from the hands of the Tokugawa family, and his Meiji government began to reorganize the nation with enlightened modernized policies on the model of Western nations. The educational reform of the Meiji government was in fact a part of its whole Westernization policy intended to be the most effective means of coping with the existing military and industrial threat of the Western powers. It was unfortunate, however, that Japan followed the power politics of the Western powers and aimed at becoming a strong nation primarily through reliance upon military and industrial might. "A wealthy nation, a strong army" was the slogan, and the government's efforts were all centred on achieving these two supreme national aims. Thus the Westernization of Japanese education was carried out under the strong leadership of a central government with this explicit purpose and in conjunction with its whole Westernization programme in government, its judicial system, industry, commerce, military developments, and many other aspects of its national life.

After passing through the initial stage of the Restoration and particularly after the abolition of the *han* system in 1871, the political leadership of the new government fell into the hands of a small oligarchical group of bureaucrats. Their immediate purpose was to replace feudalism by a modern system based on Western practice in order to be able to compete with the West. In the same year the government ordered the abolition of *han* schools, and the Ministry of Education was established to control the nations' schools. The first job of the Ministry was to develop a national education plan.

The ideas of the new leadership may be seen in the arguments of a few leaders. As early as 1867 Iwakura Tomomi had submitted to the Imperial Court a recommendation emphasizing the importance of popular enlightenment as the basis for a strong nation, and suggesting the establishment of elementary and secondary schools throughout the country. In the same year Kido Takayoshi had also submitted a memorandum recommending general education on the grounds that without an enlightened population the country would not be able to compete with other nations. Ito Hirobumi expressed similar ideas in 1869. He suggested the establishment of universal common schools through which new knowledge of the world could reach every person in the nation. All three national leaders realized equally clearly that if a strong nation were to be built up, it would be most important to organize a national system of popular education through which the people could share in the new knowledge from the West.

On the local level, *han* were replaced by *ken,* or prefectures, and the new governors were appointed by the central government. They shared the same educational views as the central leaders and promoted the dissemination of the new education policy.

The educational reform went through several stages. In the first stage, when the foundation of the new government was not yet firm and rested on the balance of different powers, there were activities of the conservative *kokugaku* restorationists and the Confucianists who took the initiative in educational policy making. In 1868, under the name of the new government, they opened a Kogakusho, or Academy for Kokugaku Studies, and reopened *bakufu* institutions of higher learning including the Shoheiko for the Confucian studies. They were, however, too conservative to meet the educational needs of the new government. Thus they were soon thrown out of power, and these *kokugaku* and Confucian schools were closed down after only one year's existence.

Their place was taken by the group of what was called Occidentalists, most of whom had worked in the *bakufu* School of Western Studies and who remained in office with the new government. They were most active in the first decade of the new regime, when the Westernization of education was at its height. During this period they studied and translated the statute books on education in Western countries to assist the government in policy-making. They also translated Western textbooks and other reference books so that they could also be used in Japanese schools.

They were assisted in their work by a group of Western educators who were invited by the Japanese government to take up advisory posts in government offices and teaching positions in government schools and university. These foreign experts numbered about a hundred each year during this period. Many of them made a great contribution to the Westernization or modernization of Japanese education. The works of several American educators were well known, among them, for example, those of David Murray who served between 1873 and 1878 as a super-intendent holding an advisory position in the Ministry of Education and who was directly involved with the policy formation of the Ministry.

The government encouraged study abroad, and sent educators and students to Western countries. Those replaced the foreign teachers and advisors on their return from such study. When the government dispatched a mission headed by Prince Iwakura to the West between 1871 and 1873, a group of the officers from the Ministry of Education accompanied the mission and made intensive observation and gathered much information on the national systems of the Western countries.

The Fundamental Code of Education of 1872

The first comprehensive government plan was the Fundamental Code of Education of 1872, which was drafted by a committee of twelve persons including influential elements of the Occidentalists. It followed the model of the French school system. Under the Ministry of Education the whole country was divided into eight academic districts, each of which should have a university, and was further divided into thirty-two secondary school districts. A secondary school district should provide a secondary school and was subdivided into 210 elementary school districts, each of which should provide an elementary school. Normal schools should be established for training teachers for the new system.

Through this ambitious plan it was intended, as the Preamble of the Code declared, that "there shall be no community with an illiterate family, nor a family with an illiterate person". In the realization of the plan, however, a list of priority was prepared by the Ministry in which the establishment of elementary schools and the preparation of teachers were given the top priority. The Ministry prepared the course of study for the elementary schools, recommended a list of textbooks, and subsidized local government, although most of the money for establishing elementary schools was paid by the local people. In the same year the Ministry set up the Tokyo Normal School in which teachers were trained in the new content and methods of teaching under an American educator, M. M. Scott. In three years, six state normal schools were set up in various provinces, and eighty-two teacher-training centres were established by local governments.

On the local level, the prefectural governors ordered the establishment of school districts and appointed school district officers, each of whom was to supervise several school districts. The reaction to the new educational system varied among prefectures. Chikuma *ken* (now part of Nagano *ken* for example, had started the new system even before the Code was really enforced. The work of Governor Nagayama was almost legendary. He visited every part of his prefecture to encourage the establishment of elementary schools, and when he ran into financial difficulty he persuaded his officials, along with himself, to contribute a considerable amount of money from their salaries. Thus within a few years his Chikuma *ken* reached the highest enrolment of children.

The role of the school district officers in putting the new system into practice was worthy of note. In many cases they were from the upper farming strata or village official class of Tokugawa days. As we have noted earlier, they had co-operated closely with the rulers and had been active in village welfare activities including popular enlightenment. It was they who had established and maintained *terakoya* and supported the *gogaku* system. The new government also relied on them to establish the new system. Financial reliance was especially important. The new system faced financial difficulties from the outset. The government could not provide enough support, so the financial burden fell heavily on the shoulders of the local people. Therefore the attitude of influential, wealthy people in the villages was very important, and where they were active, the system developed fairly rapidly.

The operation of the new system was not, of course, carried out without resistance, active or passive, from the people. Government officials reported many complaints, illustrating how negative the people were about sending their children to schools and maintaining these schools. The financial difficulty was one of the obvious reasons. The school fees were not inconsequential for ordinary people, and the additional compulsory contributions were irksome. Above all the people seemed not to realize the value of the education provided by the new system. The new schools for their part also had shortcomings. The new school resembled the Tokugawa *gogaku,* the common school provided by the rulers, rather than *terakoya,* the voluntary common school. In other words the new schools were not voluntarily developed by the people but compulsorily enforced by the central authority. The content of the new education was also in most cases alien to the daily life of the ordinary villagers since it was a direct imitation of elementary schools in the West.

Thus, despite the forceful encouragement of the government, the rate of school attendance was not much different from that of the later Tokugawa period until a few decades later when the content of education became nationalized and politico-economic necessity forced the people to send their children to school. Under such circumstances it was not surprising that peasants rioting against the new government's tax policy in the early Meiji often burnt school buildings along with police stations and town halls.

After ten years of the operation of the Code, Japan possessed 29,081 elementary schools, 194 secondary schools, 71 higher schools, and 1 university. The number of elementary schools was almost the same as that of the present day. Unfortunately there is no comparative figure on the Tokugawa *terakoya,* and therefore we cannot see statistically the difference between Tokugawa and Meiji schools. From local examples, however, we can learn how the transformation occurred.

In the first place, where no educational institutions had existed formerly, new schools were set up either in new school buildings or in private houses or public buildings. In the second place, where there had been *terakoya, shijuku,* or *gogaku,* they were either all or partly transformed into new schools without much change or they were completely abolished, and in their place a new system built, either in new school buildings or in old houses. Existing buildings, such as temples and private houses, were most commonly used, and comparatively few new school buildings were erected. Most elementary schools had one or two teachers with an average of eighty pupils. Thus, as far as the organization and buildings were concerned, there was not much difference between the Tokugawa *terakoya* and Meiji schools at this stage.

Teaching in the new elementary schools was not efficient. In 1876, out of 52,262 teachers only 6450, or about one-sixth, had been trained in new normal schools. The majority of the rest were former *terakoya* teachers who could not effectively handle the new curricula.

With regard to the secondary and higher institutions, only a few developments occurred in this period. Former *han* schools were abolished by government order in 1872. The new secondary schools were mostly private, either transformed from Tokugawa *shijuku* or newly established. The real development did not occur until toward the end of the nineteenth century. Three of the *bakufu* schools (Shoheiko, Igakusho, and Bansho-torishirabejo which was later renamed Kaiseiko) were, after several reforms, transformed into the University of Tokyo, which was later renamed the Imperial University of Tokyo. Several government technical schools were newly built, but the development of higher education also did not occur until later.

Revision of the Earlier Policies

The plan was apparently overly ambitious even though the government could draw upon the educational achievements of the previous period. In 1879 the plan was replaced by a more moderate one, and the subsequent history of government policy in education was one of adjustment and readjustment. After half a century of further development, Japan had accomplished more than the plan of 1872 intended. By 1922 there were 6 imperial universities, 20 non-imperial universities, 235 other higher institutions, 1604 secondary schools, and 25,582 elementary schools.

This remarkable achievement was accomplished by the following process. To implement the 1872 plan the government issued in that year a list of priorities in which the development of elementary education and of normal schools for elementary teachers were given first place. For the first ten years of the plan the government concentrated its limited resources upon the development of elementary education. At the same time the government created a few model institutions for secondary and higher education. In 1877 the University of Tokyo was set up, based on bakufu schools for Western studies and Western medicine, and several exemplary secondary schools both for boys and girls were established in the same period. It was expected that while the government emphasized elementary education, private efforts would stimulate the secondary and higher levels. In fact, in this period a number of private institutions were established, and these supplemented the government's limited efforts to produce an educated élite in society.

In the late 1880s the government turned its efforts to secondary education for, by this time, their earlier work in public elementary education had produced enough elementary school graduates for secondary education. The job of the government in the 1890s was to set up standard regulations for the setting up of public secondary schools and to control the existing and new private secondary schools. The same process was applied to the development of higher education which began later in the 1920s. By that time there were enough secondary school graduates to proceed to higher education and to other educational activities at higher levels. The government then laid down regulations to control the entire higher education structure and greatly expanded government higher institutions.

It must be noted that throughout the whole period of development the strong leadership of the central government was maintained, and that the objective of education was always to contribute to national strength. Mori Arinori, Minister of Education from 1885 to 1889, who was one of the great architects of the national education system, stated that education was not for the sake of individuals but for the sake of the State. According to such a philosophy there were few opportunities for individual or local initiative. Every policy and all the details were planned and regulated by the central government.

After the period of overwhelming Westernization, which ended around the end of the 1870s, the policy of separation between "Western techniques and Eastern morals" was set up and carefully maintained by the government. The traditional *kokugaku* and Confucian schools came back to the scene of national politics in education. The Occidentalists themselves began to take more the line of nationalistic thought. The Westernization of education was allowed to proceed only within the limits of technology and related practice, that is the curriculum structure, teaching methods, school organization, etc. The "moral" aims of education were cautiously prescribed and interpreted through the traditional national philosophy, the most elaborated expression of which is to be found in the Imperial Rescript on Education of 1890.

The Rescript was a joint work of Motoda Nagazana, a Confucian tutor of the Imperial Court, and Inowe Kowashi, an Occidental jurist—statesmen. It was issued in the name of the Meiji emperor and stated the objectives of education in terms of nationalist—Confucianist values. It stressed the glory of the nation and the Confucian moral concepts of loyalty, filial piety, and obedience to superiors, and this constituted the sacred national moral doctrine until the end of World War II. Thus, in spite of the overwhelming Westernization in almost every material aspect of national life, such concepts as "liberalism" and "individualism" did not enter Japanese education.

The only exception was for the short period of liberalization in education which occurred in the first and second decades of the century as a result of the influences of the worldwide liberal movement after World War I. During this period, many ideas and practices of the new education of the West were introduced and adopted by Japanese educators. Such private progressive schools as Sawayanagi's Seijo School and Obara's Tamagawa School were set up during this period as a result of the new education.

Though this new education movement brought a breath of fresh air to Japanese education, its influence was rather limited, in the first place to the large cities where most of the middle class, who were able to accept the new liberal ideas, lived, and, in the second place, to teaching methods and techniques. In other words, the majority of Japanese schools were left untouched by this movement and, above all, the aim of national education was little affected by it. Then in the 1930s, when the movement was directed toward militarism and ultra-nationalism, this liberal movement in education was suppressed and disappeared from the scene.

EDUCATION FOR INDUSTRIALIZATION

From the time that the Meiji government got into power there was a close relationship between two policies for educational advancement and industrial progress which apparently contributed to the rapid development of Japanese education as well as to the quick industrialization of Japan. Japan was by no means a planned society, but, nevertheless, there was a great deal of planning in various fields of national life, particularly in schools and industry. As to industrial planning, immediately after 1868, the government took the initiative in establishing and expanding industry. It was clear to them that a non-industrial pre-modern Japan could not compete with the Western economic and military powers.

There were several ministries which were concerned with industrial development, among them the Ministry of Industry, which was primarily responsible for government industrial planning. During its existence from 1870 to 1885 this Ministry established and maintained factories, mines, railways, telegraph system, lighthouses, dockyards, and various other industrial and technical activities of the government. Some of these enterprises resulted from direct government investment, while others were established as models and later sold to private industrialists. In this way the development of Japanese industry accelerated rapidly.

As to the manpower required for the new industry, Japan already possessed a class of craftsmen who had the skills required for the initial stage of industrialization. A new class of managers, technologists, and technicians had to be produced, however, and the government made provision for that. In 1871 the Ministry of Industry set up a College of Technology which offered courses for the training of technologists as well as for technicians. In 1886 the former was transformed into the School of Engineering of the Imperial University of Tokyo: the latter became an independent technical school. By 1890 several other technical schools had been established by the government, including schools of commerce, foreign languages, agriculture, and mercantile marine. There were also some twenty-five technical schools maintained by local authorities and private individuals or organizations which were stimulated by government activities.

As observed earlier, the Ministry of Education concentrated its efforts in the 1870s and 1880s on universal elementary education. Then in the 1890s it began to pay more attention to the organization and development of secondary and technical education. This occurred simultaneously with the progress of Japanese industry, which, helped by political stability and government encouragement, had entered the stage of what is called "take off". Between 1893 and 1899 a series of regulations on secondary and technical education was formulated by the Ministry of Education with the intention of expanding these stages of education.

By 1903 Japan had succeeded in establishing along with some 340 academic secondary schools, 200 technical schools at the secondary level, including 28 engineering, 52 commercial, 113 agricultural and fishery, and 7 mercantile marine schools. There were also some 200 part-time supplementary schools for craftsmen and apprentices. As to the post-secondary level of technical education, there were 3 engineering, 2 commercial, and 3 agricultural colleges, as well as 2 imperial universities, each of which had a school of engineering.

The same process evolved in 1920 when the industrialization of Japan moved closer to its maturity with the development of modern light techniques and Eastern morals was set up and carefully maintained by the government. The traditional *kokugaku* and Confucian incentive for such a development, and later, through the period of global depression, the incentive was provided by increased government planning, military expansion, and rationalization of the industrial sector.

This industrial development coincided with the rise of the bourgeois democracy in Japan. As a result of the earlier industrialization and educational policies of the government, which was in the hands of the enlightened autocratic-bureaucracy, a new class of industrial bourgeois emerged. By the turn of the century they had become a political power, claiming participation in government. By 1918 the first "party government" was formed under Premier Hara, and in 1928 the first general election was held under universal male suffrage, signifying the peak of bourgeois democracy. This, however, coincided with the beginning of the period of economic crisis which was affected by the panic throughout the world, and it led to both internal and external tension.

The increasing participation of the industrial class in the formation of national policy in education could be seen in their representation on the government's advisory councils, particularly on those existing between 1913 and 1935. It should be mentioned that throughout the whole period 1896 to 1942 the councils were dominated by those representing the interests of traditional bureaucracy in education who never yielded to other groups including the industrial group, even at the time of the rise of bourgeois democracy. Thus the liberalization of education, which found some supporters among the industrial class in the post-World-War-I period, was never accepted by the councils as national policy, and instead the traditional nationalistic education was reinforced during this period.

On the other hand, these bureaucratic and industrial groups shared certain common interests particularly with regard to the policy of educational expansion for industrial progress. Thus the expansion of higher education from both government and private initiative, which was of prime concern to the industrial group, was acceptable to the bureaucracy, as it was generally in accordance with the traditional policy for national strength. The industrialists, for their part, tended to follow the traditional policy of the bureaucracy for nationalistic education, hoping to produce a class of tame labourers, particularly as the tension of industrial relation increased.

Expansion of Higher Education

In 1918 the Extraordinary Conference on Education, an advisory council held from 1917 to 1919, made a recommendation, among others, on higher education, opening the way for its greater expansion. Considering various suggestions made inside and outside present and previous councils, the Conference recommended the setting up, along with the traditional multiple-faculty imperial universities, of single-faculty government universities, and the approval of private and public (prefectural and municipal) universities with both multiple- and single-faculty organization.

The recommendation was accepted by the government, and became reality under Premier Hara and his government as the University Code of 1918. In the following year the Minister of Education, Nakahashi Tokugoro, a business man, launched a six-year plan for the expansion of higher education, which was to double the number of students by establishing new state colleges and universities and by expanding the existing ones.

In ten years the number of the state higher institutions and of the students at these institutions more than doubled, and the expansion continued further with nearly the same pace. Before the expansion policy of 1918, there were 5 imperial universities with some 9000 students and 38 state colleges with 21,000 students. By 1938 the numbers had increased to 6 imperial universities and 12 government universities of technology, commerce, medicine, education, and Shinto theology, with a total of 23,000 students, and 87 state colleges of various specialities with 45,000 students.

Worthy of note was the effect of the University Code of 1918 and the government's expansion policy in higher education on the development of public and private universities and colleges. Between 1918 and 1938 several prefectural and municipal public authorities set up 5 new public universities and added 4 colleges to the 7 which were already in existence.

While the development of public higher institutions was thus not massive, that of private universities and colleges was more impressive. In 1918 there were 63 private colleges with 34,000 students: in 1938 there were 25 private universities with 44,000 students and 120 private colleges with 80,000 students. In twenty years, therefore, the number of private institutions had increased more than three and a half times, and in the latter year it constituted nearly 60 per cent of the total number of higher institutions. In the same year the students of private universities were nearly two-thirds of the total university population, and those in private colleges were over 70 per cent of the college student population.

Thus the expansion of higher education in the 1920s and 1930s which was to meet the needs of the nation for further industrialization, was achieved to a great extent by private effort. In this respect the role of the private higher institutions may be regarded as supplementary to the role of the state ones, which were not alone able to meet the demand of the time. It is true that in a country like Japan, where the initiative in educational development was largely in the hands of the State, private and local public institutions tended to be looked on as secondary and supplementary to the state ones. On the other hand, it is fair to say that these private and local institutions played more than a supplementary role in those areas where the State was unable, or unwilling, to act.

There were at least three areas which should be mentioned. The first one was that of private enterprise in manufacturing, marketing, and banking, to which the private and public universities sent many of their graduates. As has been mentioned earlier, the prime function of the original imperial university was to produce administrators and technical experts for the government. The situation changed somewhat as the expanding private activities in business and industry led to an increasing need of university graduates. To meet such a demand, the Faculty of Law of the Imperial University of Tokyo set up in 1909 a Department of Commerce, which in 1919 became the University Faculty of Economics. In the same year the Imperial University of Kyoto also set up a Faculty of Economics. The graduates of these faculties were largely employed in private business enterprises. A similar case could be observed in other faculties, where an increasing number of graduates worked outside the government. After 1919 the newly created government universities, particularly those of commerce, sent most of their graduates to non-government occupations.

However, the number of graduates from the imperial and government universities employed in private enterprise was still limited and was not enough to satisfy demand. Public and private universities had therefore to fill this gap. After 1919, when a number of private universities were created under the University Code, many of them included faculties of economics or commerce, with the definite intention of producing students who would later work in business. Thus in 1932, according to the survey made by the Ministry of Education, some 11,600 graduates were produced by 6 imperial universities, 13 government universities, 3 public universities, and 25 private universities, each group of which shared out these graduates in the ratio of 41, 11, 2, and 46 per cent respectively. From these graduates, 3060 were employed by private companies and banks, and the ratio of these among the four groups of institutions being 28, 14, 2, and 56.

This indicates that the largest supply to private business came from the private universities. To view the picture from a different angle, out of some 5300 graduates from private universities, some 32 per cent — the largest group — were employed in private business, followed by a group of 13 per cent who worked in the government. In the case of some 4800 graduates of the imperial universities, 23 per cent were employed in the government, while 18 per cent were in private enterprise. It is interesting to note that out of a total 123 graduates entering journalism, 68 per cent were from the private universities.

The second field where the public (prefectural and municipal) and private higher institution played an important role was that of women's education. There was a strong discrimination against the female sex in the state higher institutions. Among the imperial universities, only that at Tohoku after 1913 accepted female students with full status. Another three — Hokkaido, Kyushu, and Tokyo — opened their doors to them as non-degree auditors in 1918, 1925, and 1920 respectively. In the case of Tokyo, even this system was discontinued in 1928. Two government universities of arts and sciences in Tokyo and Hiroshima, which were set up in 1929 for the training of educators, also accepted female students but only in limited numbers. Thus in 1932 a mere 8 women completed degree courses in the state universities, with an additional 3 without degrees.

The situation appeared much the same in public and private universities. In 1932 none of the 3 public universities accepted female students, and of 25 private universities, only 2 were co-educational, and 1 accepted women as auditors. As a result only 2 female graduates and 4 auditors completed the courses.

On the level of non-degree-granting colleges, however, a distinct difference could be observed between state colleges and public and private ones in connection with education for women. The state colleges as a whole were still discriminative, while other groups showed more positive attitudes. In 1932, of 77 state colleges, only 1, the Tokyo Music College, was co-educational, and 2 of the higher normal schools were for women. In contrast to this, out of 14 public colleges in the same year, 6 were for women. Of 113 private colleges, 4 were co-educational and 39 were for women only.

Four of these were affiliated to private universities, and affiliation which made it possible for the graduates of the women's colleges to continue their education in the universities. Some other independent women's colleges provided professional training for women, such as in medicine, dentistry, pharmacy, theology, education, and social work, while others offered courses for general education and womanhood. Several of the pioneer colleges for women were founded in the decade of the College Code of 1903, but more than half were set up in the six years between 1925 and 1930, a period when the tide of post-World-War-I democracy was at its peak. In 1926 a National Assembly was called for the promotion of higher education for women. It was also in this period that most of the public women's colleges mentioned earlier were set up.

The third field was religious education or education based on religion. The state universities and colleges were founded as and remained secular institutions, although after 1930 this secularism was coloured by the government's introduction of pseudo-religious Shintoism which will be dealt with later. In this respect, the public higher institutions were the same as the state ones. The private universities and colleges, however, were free from this restriction. While some of the important ones were secular, other equally important groups of private institutions had religious foundations of Christiantity, Buddhism, or Shintoism. A few of them were strictly theological, and intended to train the priests of the particular religious sects, while most of these religious institutions provided the courses, together with or without the theological one, for broad professional and general education based on the educational philosophies of the different religions.

It should be added that not only in the case of religious institutions, but also in the case of secular ones, the private universities and colleges succeeded in developing their unique academic characters, which were often associated with the philosophies or beliefs of their founders. This made a contrast with the impersonal character prevailing among the state institutions in general.

EDUCATION IN THE CRISIS AND WAR

Thus in the twenties and thirties, Japanese higher education underwent a great expansion in order to meet the need of the society. It was ironical, therefore, that in the same period some of the graduates of these higher institutions had to face for the first time in Japanese history of higher education the problem of unemployment. This might be attributable at least in part to the rapid expansion of higher education itself, but the main cause was the economic situation of the time, in which business and industry began to suffer from the constant panics.

It was also in this period that the short-lived pre-World-War-II Japanese labour movement was at its peak. The national federations of the trade unions, which were organized in the early twenties, systematically led the labourers and peasants into strikes and other agitation. A few political parties associated with the labour movement were organized in this period by groups of various sects of socialists and communists. Among them, the Communist Party, which was secretly organized in 1922, was declared illegal and suppressed by the government. Other socialist parties and the labour movement led by them also suffered to various degrees from government pressure.

Influenced by such general unrest in society and also by the rise of the movements against the *status quo,* the student agitation arose in the campuses. The first student movement started in 1918 within the Imperial University of Tokyo and spread to other institutions. By 1922 it had organized a national federation of socialist students, and begun to concern itself more positively with the problems both inside and outside the campus. As the government strengthened its oppressive control over the socialist movements, the student movement became more radical and as a consequence suffered more from the government. Between 1926 and 1930 many of its leaders were arrested and various organizations were ordered to be dissolved.

Schools did not remain untouched by social unrest. The socialist movement, which was anti *status quo,* was also critical of the existing situation in schools. During the labour disputes in the twenties there were some cases in which the labourers or peasants sent their children to the "proletarian schools". Between 1929 and 1933 a few attempts were made to organize teachers' unions, and as a part of the movement a short-lived Proletarian Education Institute was set up as a centre for the socialist education movement. This soon met government oppression. Together with the leaders of this movement, many individuals and groups of school teachers, who intended to liberalize school education, were suppressed on suspicion of being "red". This was a blow to the post-World-War-I liberal education movement, which soon ceased its activities.

As liberalism retreated, nationalism in education came forward in the government's policies in the thirties, partly to counteract the socialism and liberalism prevailing among students, teachers, and intellectuals. More positively, it was also meant to unify the people ideologically for the possible forthcoming war preparations. In political circles the power was shifted from the hands of bourgeois democrats to that of right-wing nationalists and the military. The latter group brought the nation to war with China in 1937 after a series of minor military incidents in the early thirties, and, finally, to total war in the Pacific in 1941.

In 1932 the Ministry of Education established an Institute for the Study of National Moral Culture, which functioned till the end of World War II as an ideological centre of nationalistic Japan. In 1934 the Bureau of Thought was created within the Ministry for thought control. In 1935 the Ministry called the Council for Renovating Education and Learning, which in the following year made its recommendations including the encouragement of higher learning in Japanese history and morals and the reform of school education on nationalistic lines. One of the results of the recommendations was the Ministry's effort to establish a chair of Japanese national morals in each of the imperial universities of Tokyo and Kyoto and in the two government universities of arts and science in Tokyo and Hiroshima.

Another result was the establishment in 1937 of the new Education Council, which was to review the school system for the reform on nationalistic lines. The Council's reports, which were made between 1938 and 1941, covered all aspects of national education and gave new directions to Ministry policies in subsequent years.

The first measure which the Ministry of Education took in 1939, following the Council's recommendations, was to make boys' attendance in youth schools compulsory up to the age of 19. The youth schools, the origins of which go back partly to the supplementary vocational schools established in 1893 and partly to the youth training centres established in 1926, were set up in 1935 to provide supplementary general and vocational education for working boys and girls. For boys, military training was also given. It was evidently with the military necessity in mind that the attendance of working boys in youth schools was made compulsory up to the age of conscription.

The second measure was the reform of elementary schools, which in 1941 were renamed "national schools", with the corresponding change in curriculum. All school subjects were to be integrated into the principles of nationalistic education. The courses in the national schools extended over eight years, and the school-leaving age was to be raised from 12 to 14 by 1944, although this was postponed indefinitely by the outbreak of the Pacific war.

The third measure was concerned with the reorganization of secondary education. Three kinds of schools, middle schools for boys, girls' high schools, and vocational schools, which were hitherto differentiated from each other, were given equal status by the Secondary School Ordinance of 1943, and a measure was provided to make possible the transfer of pupils between the first two kinds of schools and the last one. The curricula of secondary schools were also integrated in the same nationalistic principles as in national schools.

The fourth measure was on the training of elementary or national school teachers. In 1943 the status of normal schools was elevated from the level of secondary school to that of college, receiving students from among the graduates of middle schools or girls high schools. The training course extended over three years. At the same time, the administration of normal schools was handed over from the prefectures to the State, thus giving the new normal schools the status of the government colleges.

The report of the Education Council in 1941 dealt with social education or education outside school. Up to that time this area of education had been neglected, but the preparation for total war necessitated its expansion under the government's initiative. In the same year a national federation was organized under government auspices for the social and educational activities of children and young people. In the following year a similar national organization was set up for married women.

These measures to reorganize the educational system of the nation were in fact greatly impeded by the progress of the Pacific war. This was particularly true in the case of higher education. The Council's report of 1940 suggested several measures for improving the quality of research and education in universities and colleges. While some of them were put into practice by the government, the progress of the war required the introduction of certain emergency measures which had a reverse effect on higher education.

In 1941 an ordinance was issued to decrease the length of higher education to meet manpower demand, and by 1943 the courses in universities and colleges were shortened by nearly two-thirds. In the same year the government decided to discontinue the temporary exemption from enlistment of arts students, and sent a large number of those over conscription age into military service. At the same time teaching in arts was drastically cut down, and the number of arts students was reduced by one-third. The students in universities and colleges as well as in the secondary schools were to spend at least one-third of their time in factories or farms or in auxiliary war services. The last measure was further strengthened in 1944, when the students were expected to work in war services all the year round.

In 1945, when the mainland of Japan was constantly under severe air attack, regular schooling became almost impossible. School buildings were either destroyed or utilized for war services. Children in large cities were forced to evacuate to the country. Young male teachers were all in military service. In March 1945 the government, almost in despair, declared an emergency in national education, by which all schooling except in national schools was to be suspended temporarily to prepare the nation for the forthcoming final battle on the mainland. Japanese national education had thus been already defeated by this educational *harakiri* before two atomic bombs brought the tragic war to a miserable end for the people of Japan in August 1945.

EDUCATION DURING THE OCCUPATION AND AFTER

Japan was occupied by the Allies between August 1945 and April 1952, during which time its education underwent a radical change. The policies of the occupation were guided by the Potsdam Declaration which was issued on 26 July 1945 to specify the conditions of the Japanese surrender. It required the Japanese to eliminate the leaders who had deceived and misled the people into war and to remove the obstacles to the revival and strengthening of democratic tendencies among the Japanese people. The occupying forces were to be withdrawn when a peace-inclined and responsible government was established in accordance with the freely expressed will of the Japanese people.

The initiative of the occupation was in the hands of the government of the United States, who through their occupying army carried out these policies, i.e. demilitarization and democratization in all aspects of government and life of the Japanese including education. The details of the policies on education were formulated in the General Headquarters of the Supreme Commander of the Allied Powers, in which a staff section called Civil Information and Education (CIE) was responsible for educational matters. In the process of forming policies, the *ad hoc* commissions of specialists were invited from their home countries. Among them, the most important was a United States Education Mission invited in March 1946. After one month of study, the Mission submitted a report which provided a policy guide for the occupation authority as well as for the Japanese government.

The Japanese government was to implement the policies laid down by the occupation authority under the close supervision of the latter's headquarters and the American Military Government teams stationed in each of the forty-six prefectures. The degree of closeness in supervision changed as the occupation progressed, and in its later stage the execution of the details was left more in the hands of the Japanese.

On the Japanese side, the major instruments for educational reform were the Ministry of Education and the Educational Reform Council. Despite the decentralization policy of the occupation authority, which will be described later, the Ministry continued to exist in the same form as before, and functioned during the whole period of the occupation almost as sole administrative organ for the implementation and dissemination of the directives of the occupation authority throughout the country. The Educational Reform Council started as a Japanese education committee, a counterpart body to the United States Education Mission, provided by the latter with technical advice. The Council's function was to study the suggestions made by the United States Education Mission and to make concrete recommendations to the Prime Minister. The Council worked independently, but it was "advised" by a steering committee composed of three members each from the Council, the Ministry, and the Education Division of the CIE. During its existence between September 1946 and June 1952, the Council held 142 general meetings and 350 subcommittee meetings and made 35 recommendations, many of which were subsequently put into practice by the parliamentary enactments and Ministry enforcement.

The first phase of the occupation policy, i.e. demilitarization of Japanese education, was almost completed by the end of 1946. The measures taken in this period included the abolition of the wartime emergency regulations by the Ministry and the putting into force of four directives of the Supreme Commander concerning the elimination of military and ultranationalistic elements in teaching, the removal from public office of the wartime leaders in education, the separation of the Shinto religion from the State, and the suspension of the courses in morals, Japanese history, and geography.

By the end of 1949 a series of enactments in the National Diet provided the groundwork for the second phase of the occupation policy, i.e. the democratization of Japanese education, on which a new democratic system of national education was to be established. Only brief mention of these measures will be made here, as they will be discussed in more detail in later chapters.

In March 1946 the first and most important legislation, the Fundamental Law of Education, was enacted. The Law provided for the new educational system the basic principles which had hitherto been provided by the Imperial Rescript on Education. The proclamation of the Fundamental Law set up an important precedent by which all major education regulations were hereafter made through parliamentary procedure. These regulations or laws replaced the Imperial Ordinances, which had regulated the pre-war educational system. The Imperial Rescript on Education was nullified by the National Diet in May 1948.

The School Education Law of March 1947 laid down a new system of the so-called 6—3—3—4 single ladder, in the place of the pre-war system of multiple tracks. The school-leaving age was raised from 12 to 15 years. Co-education was encouraged throughout the whole system. The new school system was put into operation on 1 April 1947 when new elementary and middle schools were started. New high schools were started in the following year. Reorganization of higher education was a little delayed. A dozen private universities were started under the new system in 1948, but most of the new universities, including the state ones, began in 1949.

The operation of the new school system was not without difficulty. Wartime loss, which amounted to 13 per cent of the total school building, and also the raising of the school-leaving age, which increased the number of children of compulsory attendance age by half, led to a serious shortage of school buildings and facilities, which were hard to supply under the financial constraints of the time. Overcrowded classrooms in temporary huts with double or triple shifts were not uncommon.

Prior to the operation, the new courses of study for elementary, middle, and high schools were written by the Ministry of Education. The textbooks were also prepared by the Ministry till 1949, when under a new arrangement textbooks were produced by private publishers with the Ministry's authorization. The teachers were to be reoriented in the new curricula, textbooks, and methods of teaching, and after the autumn of 1946 the Ministry of Education and local authorities organized a series of re-education programmes for teachers on a large scale.

In April 1949, when the Teachers' Certification Law was issued, teachers in service were put under the ten-year scheme of the Ministry of Education to be further trained to meet the higher requirements for the new teachers' certificates. The Law required all teachers to have the qualification of the four-year college graduates, although two-year college education or its equivalent was temporarily accepted. The normal schools were to be reorganized to cope with the new requirement for incoming teachers, and in May of the same year they were either incorporated into the newly established state universities or became independent colleges of education.

The reorganization of normal schools was a part of the reform of higher education in general, which took place mostly in the period between 1948 and 1950. By this reform the total 658 higher institutions were re-organized into 201 universities of four-year courses, with the exception of the six-year medical and dental courses, and into 150 two- or three-year junior colleges. Some of the universities were expected to develop post-graduate courses later.

In June 1949 the Social Education Law was enacted, which among other things legalized the establishment of community halls that had been already developing since 1946 with the encouragement of the Ministry.

All these reforms in school and adult education were accompanied by the reorganization of educational administration which was directed toward its decentralization. The traditional centralized structure was first broken up by the promulgation of the Board of Education Law in July 1948, which required all local communities, both prefectures and municipalities, to have the popularly elected boards of education. The boards were responsible for establishing and maintaining schools, determining curricula, choosing textbooks, buying instructional materials, and providing in-service training for teachers. The prefectural boards were given additional power to certify teachers, approve textbooks, and provide technical and professional advice and guidance for municipal boards. In October 1948 the first election was held and the boards of education were set up in forty-six prefectures and five big cities. In the election in October 1952 the boards were also established in some 10,000 other municipalities.

The role of the Ministry of Education now changed. The Ministry of Education Establishment Law of May 1949 defined the primary function of the Ministry as advisory and stimulating. Its internal structure was reorganized accordingly.

The democratization of Japanese education was thus carried out by the Japanese themselves, who were, however, under the direction of the American occupation authority. This fact was responsible for certain major characteristics of the reform. For one thing, it was "forced" democratization under the military occupation. It is true that in the execution of the democratization policy the occupation authority adopted democratic procedure as much as they could, and that many Japanese were stimulated and enlightened by the democracy and were positively committed to the democratic reform of education. On the other hand, it is equally true that it was hard for a democratic relationship to exist between the occupier and the occupied, and that democratization of education was passively accepted by many Japanese as a result of the defeat and as a necessity to restore the independence of the nation.

There was also the question of time. From the viewpoint of both the occupation authority and the Japanese, the occupation was not to continue indefinitely, and thus the democratization of Japan should be achieved in a fairly short length of time. Consequently, while the democratization progressed fairly quickly on the formal and legal side of the educational system, a question remained as to whether the same progress was made in the democratic consciousness of the people on which any formal reform should be based.

The reform was an example of educational transplantation in which a system of education of a country is transplanted to another country with a different social and cultural background. The American ideas and practices of democratic education were introduced by the occupation authority as models for the democratic education in Japan. Little consideration was given to the differences in social and cultural backgrounds of the two countries. The American models were presented as ideals, often minimizing the problems in reality and the difficulties in transplantation. On the Japanese side, the mechanism of reinterpretation, selection, and even partial rejection worked in the process of this transplantation, and when they were transplanted to Japanese soil the American models underwent some modification irrespective of the intention of the introducer.

Some of the American models for democratic education were accepted by the Japanese more completely than others. Generally those which could remain in the abstract and general level, such as basic principles of the democratic system of education and the teaching of democratic values, were relatively well received, although one could rightly doubt whether the acceptance in such cases might not be superficial.

Difficulties arose when the matters were more on the concrete and particular level. Among them, however, those which were known to the Japanese from past experience were naturally received more easily than others. Thus, such policies as the raising of the school-leaving age and the reorganization of lower secondary education following the American pattern were carried out immediately by the Japanese despite the financial difficulties which might otherwise have been used as an excuse for sabotage. There was also a trend towards an easy acceptance of changes in matters that could more or less be confined within school, such as the reform of curricula and teaching methods.

On the other hand, matters which were unfamiliar to the Japanese and which still required the positive voluntary support of the people, were not easily accepted. The best example of this was the decentralization of educational administration, which had been alien to the Japanese since 1870. The boards of education did not find enthusiastic popular support: the voting rate in the elections did not rise beyond 56 per cent. The idea of layman control following the American model was rejected by the Japanese who elected a large number of board members from among the educators and the leaders of the teachers' unions. The political neutrality of the boards of education was hard to maintain in Japan. The Ministry of Education on its side lost much of its legal power over local authorities, but during the whole period of decentralization it maintained its central leadership through "advice and assistance" which were often sought positively by the local authorities.

Education for Independent Japan

With the end of the occupation in April 1952 the contemporary history of Japan began, and its educational problems will be discussed in the following chapters on the different topics. By way of introduction, however, it may be appropriate to make a few remarks here on some of the main themes of Japanese education in the 1950s and 1960s.

One of the main themes is democratization of education, which was "given" during the occupation. The independence of Japan provided the Japanese with an opportunity to make this democratization their own. Indeed, one may summarize these twenty years of Japanese education as a process of effort to make this "transplanted" democratic education take root in Japanese soil. How far it has been successful is still a matter of debate and hard to judge. One thing is clear, however; their success may not be measured by the set model of democratic education, American or of any other kind. Instead of adopting the ready-made model, the Japanese people have been seeking after their own model of democratic education, through the painful process of trial and error, in meeting their problems.

Among the problems to be confronted in this process was a question of nationalism. As observed earlier, nationalism was one of the main forces of building a Japanese nation and its national system of education after the latter part of the nineteenth century. However, the excessive nationalism in the 1930s and later 1940s brought the nation misery and humiliation. During most of the occupation period, nationalism was almost taboo to the people, particularly in the field of education. Instead of particular national values which were often labelled as feudalistic or reactionary, emphasis was given to the universal values, among which democracy was given priority. Thus nationalism and democracy were conceived as two values contradicting each other. When Japan got independence and a search for new national identity began, it was this dilemma that was to be solved first. The establishment of a new nationalism which is compatible with democracy has, however, been a hard process. This is particularly true in education.

Another problem was on the control of education. For the first time in the history of Japan, education was given into the hands of the people, who were to exercise their power through the decentralized system of educational administration on the American model. The independence of Japan gave a chance to the Japanese to consider whether this system should continue in the present form or not.

In this regard, the role of the Ministry of Education, whose authority was legally minimized but in practice remained as before, was most important. There is no doubt that behind the rapid development of the national system of the pre-war Japan and even behind the swift reform during the occupation, there was an efficient administrative machinery of the Ministry of Education. The efficiency in administration was further required later, when Japan launched the expansion of its education, particularly in the 1960s. Then the problem for the Japanese would be how to create a mechanism of administration, in which two principles — popular control and administrative efficiency — should be compatible.

Another educational theme for independent Japan was concerned with the relationship between education and economic or industrial development. The theme was, of course, not new to Japan. As observed earlier, education and industry, stimulating and contributing to each other, made almost parallel progress from the last part of the nineteenth century. During the occupation, this aspect was mostly neglected in the formation of educational policy, perhaps because of the uncertainty of the economic future of Japan at the time. The independence of Japan had to be accompanied with the independence of Japanese economy and industry. It was therefore natural that, with the independence of Japan, attention should be given to the role of education in the recovery and progress of Japanese economy.

After the middle of the 1950s, when the Japanese economy underwent unprecedented expansion, education was once more effectively used as an instrument for industrial progress. Reorganization and expansion of secondary and higher education in this period were considered to meet primarily the needs of this expanding economy. This, however, raised concern among some people that education was excessively subject to economy and led to the controversy on the government's policy of education and industry.

The third theme was popularization of education. In the years following the occupation, the opportunity for education was further extended. The way to this expansion was first made clear by the democratization policies during the occupation, such as the raising of the school-leaving age, the reorganization of the school system into a single-ladder type, the encouragement of co-education, and the promotion of adult education. In general, these policies were matched with the people's aspiration for education, which was already in the pre-wartime one of the driving forces of educational expansion. After the occupation, such aspiration was further stimulated by the recovery and progress of the Japanese economy, which not only provided the nation with the material basis for educational expansion but also demanded on their side highly educated manpower in great quantity.

The expansion of educational opportunity in the post-war period was, of course, not without difficulty. The forms and methods through which the expansion was to be carried out were always points of controversy. There was such a pathological phenomenon as the excessive domination of college entrance preparation in school programmes, for which the people's enthusiasm might be partly to blame. There were groups of children who were less favoured than others in their opportunities in education by their physical or social handicaps.

The extended opportunity for education was also found in the institutions outside schools, such as those within industry and adult education facilities. As they increased their activities, their integration with school education became a problem.

Finally, the popularization of education required a greater supply of qualified teachers. Various measures were taken to increase the efficiency of pre- and in-service training of teachers. At the same time, efforts were made to improve the working conditions of teachers by both education authorities and teachers' unions. The latter also concerned themselves increasingly with the policy questions on education in general, and became an influential power in deciding on the future course of national education in Japan.

Note: Part of Chapters 2 and 3 appeared in the author's "Tokugawa Education as a Foundation of Modern Education in Japan", *Comparative Education Review*, Vol. IX, No. 3, 1965, pp. 288–302.

CHAPTER 3

Principles of National Education

A system of national education operates under certain principles which, while reflecting the goals and ideals of the nation, define the purposes and policy guidelines for its operation. Under the Japanese system such principles are found in the first place in such statutes as the 1946 Constitution of Japan and the 1947 Fundamental Law of Education. They are legally expressed principles concerning the rights and responsibilities in national education which have been set up by the people through parliamentary processes and are legally binding on the government as well as on the people of Japan. All other educational laws and regulations are derived from such legal principles prescribed in these two basic laws. Not all nations provide themselves with legal principles of national education, therefore the case of Japan should be explained in its historical and socio-political context.

In this connection it must be remembered that, although the importance of statutory principles in guiding national education is unquestionable, these legal principles are not solely responsible for its direction. There are other political, economic, social, and cultural principles which have equally important effects upon national education. These factors outside education have exercised influence, not only in the process of formulating the statutory principles of national education, but also on the interpretation and execution of the principles thus established.

It is not, however, the main purpose of this chapter to go into the details of this question. There will be other chapters which deal with the problems of national education in relation to politics, economics, and society respectively. In this chapter an attempt will be made only to explain the establishment of statutory principles of national education in an historical and socio-political context, and to examine the problems connected with the aims of national education which have been under the influence of not only statutory provisions but also various other factors in Japanese society.

PRINCIPLES OF NATIONAL EDUCATION UNDER THE MEIJI CONSTITUTION

Until August 1945, when Japan came under the occupation, Japan had been ruled for more than half a century under the 1889 Constitution of the Greater Empire of Japan, or the so-called Meiji Constitution. This Constitution was drawn up by the oligarchical bureaucracy who led the Meiji Restoration, and whose main concern was to unify the nation under the new leadership and make it strong and rich enough to meet the imperialistic threat of Western powers. In the process of the political struggle through which the new Meiji government had replaced the old feudalistic war-lord government, the age-honoured Emperor had been found to be the most effective authority under which the nation could be unified.

Thus the Constitution of 1889, which attempted to lay down the foundations of the new government, was promulgated in the name of the Emperor, and gave him absolute power. According to the mythology which had been believed for centuries, the emperor's sovereignty had been established by the Imperial Founder and passed on by inheritance, and was to be inherited by the Imperial lineage unbroken, for time immemorial. These beliefs became a constitutional doctrine forming the essential nature of the national policy or *kokutai* in Japanese usage.

The Meiji Constitution attempted two things: on the one hand, it aimed to establish the absolute authority of the Emperor and his government over the people, and, on the other hand, it guaranteed the minimum of civil rights to permit the people to engage in the civic and economic activities necessary for the building of the nation for industrial development. The latter was, however, allowed only in so far as it did not impede the former.

The sovereign's benevolent rule was to be administered by his ministers of state, and he legislated with the consent of the Imperial Diet, consisting of two houses, in which the people, or rather his subjects, were given limited representation. The powers of the Diet were further limited by the constitutional provisions which recognized a wide range of Imperial prerogatives, which were carried out, not through the laws, but by Imperial ordinances.

It was thus considered that national education aimed, firstly, at training the subjects in loyalty to the Emperor and the State, and, secondly, at giving them the knowledge and skills necessary for their civic and economic activities which were to be motivated by their loyalty and patriotism. Thus education was regarded primarily as the affair of the State, or of the Emperor and his government. This idea was taken for granted when the Meiji Constitution was formulated, and thus even without mentioning it specifically in the Constitution, national education was exclusively under the Imperial prerogative, by means of which the Emperor carried out his traditional function of enlightening the people by his divine virtue and benevolence.

Thus all educational regulations until 1945 were issued as Imperial Ordinances in the name of the Emperor, without any deliberation by the Diet. The only exceptions were those involving financial questions, which required the consent of the Diet. Occasionally the Emperor also issued Imperial Rescripts to clarify his position with regard to the principles of national education. During the period between 1880 and 1945 at least four Imperial Rescripts were promulgated, which were related to the education of the nation. They were as follows: an Imperial Rescript on Education in 1890; one on thrift and industry in 1908; one for the morality of the nation in 1923; and one addressed to the youth in 1939.

Of these, the first, i.e. the 1890 Imperial Rescript on Education, was the most important and had the most profound influence on the philosophy of national education up to 1945. This Rescript was issued in the year following the promulgation of the Meiji Constitution and in the same year as the opening of the first session of the Imperial Diet. It was quite clear that this Rescript on Education was intended to supplement the Constitution by pronouncing the Emperor's responsibility for setting the aims and principles of the nation's education.

The text of the Imperial Rescript on Education began with the declaration that national education was to be founded within the framework of *kokutai*. It read as follows:

"Our Imperial Ancestors have founded Our Empire on a basis broad and everlasting and have deeply and firmly implanted virtue; Our subjects ever united in loyalty and filial piety have from generation to generation illustrated the beauty thereof. This is the glory of the fundamental character of Our Empire, and herein also lies the source of Our education."

On the basis of this nationalistic framework of *kokutai*, further mention was made of various moral virtues, some of which such as fidelity, filial duty, obedience, and submissiveness, were derived from the Confucian moral doctrines specifically applied to the hierarchical and paternal relationship between the Emperor and his subjects, between parents and their children, between man and wife, between senior and junior, while other virtues, such as patriotism, public duty, philanthropy, observation of laws, were of a modern tone related to public ethics in social and national life. Persuance of learning and cultivation of art were also mentioned. These moral virtues were "indeed the teaching bequeathed by Our Imperial Ancestors, to be observed alike by Their Descendants and the subject infallible for all ages and true in all places", and it was the Imperial wish that the Emperor himself as well as his subjects should all attain the same virtue.

Thus the Imperial Rescript on Education not only described the items of moral value which subsequently became the substance of the moral instruction or *shushin* in the national schools, but also laid down the principle of national education which was to teach the loyal subjects their patriotic duties to guarantee the everlasting continuance of national policy or *kokutai*.

Thereafter all provisions for national education were built around this principle. Various Imperial Ordinances were issued to formulate a national system of education which was to substantiate the spirit of the Imperial Rescript on Education. Moral instruction or *shushin,* which was to amplify the content of the Rescript, was the central subject in the nation's schools, but all other subjects were also to be taught in the spirit of the Imperial Rescript. Pupils were reminded of this principle of national education not only in the classroom, but at every opportunity. The photographs of the Emperor and Empress were kept in the "shrine" on the school premises, and on national occasions or during big events at school, the pictures were moved to the school assembly hall where the Imperial Rescripts were read to the pupils on behalf of the Emperor by the school principal.

After its promulgation in 1890 the Imperial Rescript on Education served more than half a century as the moulding power of national education, and thus of the nation as well. With the wide spread of the national system of education, which by 1900 already covered the majority of the population and by 1945 certainly all of it, the spirit of the Imperial Rescript on Education, and thus the nationalistic principle of education, was firmly implanted in the heart of the populace and thus created a nation unified under the authority of the Emperor.

On the other hand, it also played an important part in centralizing the authority for educational control on the Emperor and his government, thus leaving little opportunity for the people to regard education as their own right. They were, after all, part of the whole political system centred around the authoritarian Emperor and his government, which ruled Japan until 1945.

NEW CONSTITUTION AND THE FUNDAMENTAL LAW OF EDUCATION

The Constitution of 1946, which is often called the "New Constitution" in contrast to the "old" Meiji Constitution, laid down the foundations of democratic Japan, whose sovereign power now rests in the hands of the people. The Emperor has lost all his political authority, and remains as the "symbol" of the nation. The National Diet has become the highest organ of state power and the law-making body of the State. The Constitution spelled out the rights and duties of the people. The list of the thirty articles in Chapter Three covers items which are observed in almost any democratic constitution in the world today. It includes, for example, equality under law, freedom of thought and conscience, religious freedom, freedom of assembly and speech, right of collective bargaining and employment, and the right to enjoy at least the minimum standards of living.

There is no doubt that this Constitution was formulated under pressure from the occupation authority, but it is equally true that it represented the desire of the people who had suffered from the war for which the autocratic government was responsible, and who thus hoped for a new form of government which would give them a peaceful life.

The immediate national goal was to be re-admitted to international society as a respectable member at the earliest opportunity, and it was widely understood that the only way to do this was to reform Japan into a democratic and peaceful nation and to declare, in the form of a

Constitution, its determination to rebuild the nation. Thus democracy and pacifism were the two ideals which influenced the formation of various articles in the Constitution as mentioned earlier. This was exemplified in Article 9, which renounced war as a sovereign right of the nation and the use of force as a means of settling international disputes.

In this democratic constitution, reference is made to education in the articles defining the rights and duties of the people. Article 26, above all others, specifies the right and duty of the people, as well as the duty of the State with regard to educational opportunity. It reads:

"All people shall have the right to receive an equal education according to their ability, as provided by the law. The people shall be obliged to have all boys and girls under their protection receive general education as provided by law. Such compulsory education shall be free."

Other articles are also related to education, guaranteeing equality under law (Article 14), freedom of thought and conscience (Article 19), religion and belief (Article 20), assembly and speech (Article 21), learning (Article 23), and the welfare of children (Article 27). The State is forbidden to engage in any religious activities (Article 20) and in censorship (Article 21). The State must exert itself for the improvement and enrichment of social welfare, social security, and public health (Article 25). The civil service is to serve the whole people, and not its parts (Article 15).

Thus the Constitution of 1946 has made two points very clear with regard to the education of the nation, points which provide a marked contrast to the nature of national education under the Meiji Constitution. The first point is that education is a right that the people possess innately. It is no longer regarded as something that is given to them by the Emperor or the State and must, therefore, be observed as the obligation of the people. Instead, it is the duty of the State to guarantee such rights to the people and children. This is a Copernican change in the concept of national education which the people of Japan had never experienced before.

The second point is contained in the axiom following the first point, that is to say that it is not the Imperial Rescripts but the wishes of the people which should define the purposes and nature of education that the people should receive as its right.

These points immediately raised a question as to the validity of the Imperial Rescript on Education under the New Constitution. A point put forward in favour of the Imperial Rescript was that it contained moral values which transcended time and that therefore it should remain, regardless of the nature of the government. It was also argued that if the Imperial Rescript on Education became outdated under the New Constitution, a new Rescript should be issued. These arguments were fairly widely expressed and supported by some of the influential figures in post-war Japanese education, including three ministers of education, appointed consecutively from 1945 to 1948. This fact shows how deeply the Imperial Rescript on Education had affected the minds of the Japanese who had grown up under the old Constitution.

Upon the promulgation of the New Constitution, however, these arguments for the Imperial Rescript lost ground, and in June 1948 the National Diet confirmed that the Imperial Rescript on Education was invalid. The then Minister of Education, Tanaka Kotaro, in interpreting this parliamentary action, announced that the Imperial Rescript on Education had lost its political and legal effect on the nation's education, and would remain only as a general moral text.

Behind the arguments about the Imperial Rescript on Education was a feeling that some kind of authoritative document should be in existence to guide post-war Japanese education — a feeling which was shared not only by those supporting the use of the Imperial Rescript for this particular purpose but also by those not necessarily in favour of it. The latter sought another source of authority, and by the end of 1946 it had become common understanding that this source should be the people, represented by the National Diet. Thus in March 1947 the National Diet passed a Fundamental Law of Education which was to serve as a basis for national education in Japan under the New Constitution.

The 1947 Fundamental Law of Education consists of a preamble and eleven articles. In the preamble the aim of the Fundamental Law is declared to be to clarify the aims and principles of education for the new Japan in accordance with the spirit of the Constitution. By adopting the Constitution, the people of Japan declared their determination to establish a democratic nation and to contribute to the peace and welfare of humanity. The realization of this ideal depends very much on the kind of education the people receive, and therefore it is imperative that aims and principles of education appropriate to this purpose should be set up in the form of a law made by the representatives of the people.

Article 1 defines the aim of education as being "the full development of personality" and the training of "builders of the peaceful state and society" who "love truth and justice, esteem individual value, respect labour, have a deep sense of responsibility, and are imbued with an independent spirit". Article 2 states that such aims of education should be realized "on all occasions and in all places", and that in order to realize them, special consideration should be given to "academic freedom", "practicality of education", and "mutual respect and co-operation".

The following three articles deal with the rights of the people to receive equal opportunities in education regardless of race, creed, sex, social and economic status, or family origin, and with the duty of parents or guardians to give their children nine years' compulsory education and, finally, with the obligation of the State and local authorities to guarantee such educational opportunities.

Article 6 defines schools as public institutions which can be set up only by the State, local public bodies, and private corporations. Teachers are regarded as servants of the whole community and are to be given moral and material security appropriate to their service. Article 7 defines the duties of the State and local government with regard to the promotion of out-of-school education.

Articles 8 and 9 deal with political education and religious education respectively. Both politics and religion should be dealt with in education, but any partisan political education is forbidden in schools. Sectarian religious instruction is not allowed in public and state schools.

Article 10 declares the autonomy of education which should not be subject to any sectarian pressure, but should be responsible to the whole people. It also states that the purpose of educational administration is to adjust and establish the conditions required for the pursuit of the aim of education. Finally, Article 11 maintains that appropriate laws must be enacted to bring into effect the foregoing stipulations.

The Fundamental Law of Education laid down general principles of national education which were further defined by the various laws subsequently enacted by the National Diet. They included the School Education Law of 1947, the Board of Education Law of 1948, the Ministry of Education Establishment Law of 1949, the Private School Law of 1949, and Social Education Law of 1949, the Law for the Special Regulations concerning Educational Public Service of 1949, the Law for Certification of Educational Personnel of 1949, and the Industrial Education Promotion Law of 1951.

Since Japan's independence in 1952, more laws have been enacted. Among them are the Law Governing Provisional Measures for Securing Political Neutrality of Compulsory Education of 1954, and the Law Concerning the Organization and Function of Local Educational Administration of 1956, both of which were issued amidst much controversy. During the same period, some of the laws which were enacted before 1951 have been revised, also amidst much opposition.

Except for those of a technical nature, most of the educational enactments since 1952 have been faced with constant opposition with regard to the legitimacy and validity of these enactments in the light of the principles set forth in the Fundamental Law of Education. These later developments will be discussed further in following chapters, and in this chapter mention will be made only of the problems relating to the aims of national education.

AIMS OF NATIONAL EDUCATION

One of the principles laid down by the Fundamental Law of Education was the liberation of the aims and content of education, as stated in its first two articles. It was further spelled out by the School Education Law of 1947 and the Course of Study that was published in the same period by the Ministry of Education.

The School Education Law stated the objectives of elementary education as follows:

(1) to cultivate right understanding, the spirit of co-operation and independence in connection with relationships between human beings on the basis of children's experience in social life both inside and outside the school;

(2) to develop a proper understanding of the actual conditions and traditions both of children's native communities and of the country, and further to cultivate the spirit of international co-operation;

(3) to cultivate basic understanding and skill of food, clothing, housing, industries, etc., needed in everyday life;

(4) to cultivate the ability to understand and use correctly words and expressions of the Japanese language needed in everyday life;

(5) to cultivate the ability to understand and manage correctly mathematical relations needed in everyday life;

(6) to cultivate the ability to observe and dispose of natural phenomena met with in everyday life in a scientific manner;

(7) to cultivate habits needed for a sound, safe, and happy life and to effect a harmonious development of mind and body;

(8) to cultivate basic understanding and skill in music, fine arts, literature, etc., which make life bright and rich.

Similar consideration was given by the School Education Law to the objectives of secondary education, which were adjusted to the mental and physical development of pupils as well as to their needs.

The Course of Study described in detail new school curricula and teaching methods, and also sought to define the aims and objectives of new education in terms of actual educational practices in school. On the whole, the Course of Study, published around 1947, put heavy emphasis on free development of the individual, although it did not neglect to mention the social aspect of individual development. A child develops his personality through various experiences, and above all through free contact with other members of a society. Thus, becoming a good citizen was regarded almost as synonymous with becoming a man, and for this reason a new subject, social studies, occupied a significant part of the school curricula. This subject was intended to train the child in the knowledge, skills, and attitudes necessary for becoming a good citizen. A child was to learn how to live in his surrounding community, which expands as he grows up to take in his peer group, local society, the State, and eventually the world community, according to his age.

On the whole, universalistic qualities in personality which would be relevant in any kind of society, were given much emphasis, while particularistic ones which might apply only to one particular kind of society, were not given much attention. This was already observed in the statement of the aims of education in the Fundamental Law of Education, which includes such phrases as "sound in mind and body", "truth and justice", "individual values", "a deep sense of responsibility", "an independent spirit", and so on. Similar words with a universalistic tone were used repeatedly in other documents in describing the aims and objectives of education.

This was a reflection of the "spirit of the time" in the post-war period of Japan, when universalism was accepted as a reaction against the particularism which had prevailed so much during the nationalistic period until the end of the war. The Constitution of 1947 was itself based on universalistic philosophy, and was in accord with general trends in the democratic constitutions of the world. By the same token, the Fundamental Law of Education and related documents spelled out the aims of education in the light of a general democratic philosophy of education, and thus these aims could be applied to the education of any democratic nation in the world. This is in distinct contrast to the pre-war aims of Japanese education, which were defined on particularistic, nationalistic bases.

This universalism in the aims of education had by 1952 already become a source of discontent and thus a target of criticism. The traditional way of thinking dies hard. Those who were nostalgic about the Imperial Rescript on Education still felt that the aims of education should be written somewhat in the same particularistic way as in the Imperial Rescript, and they attributed the apparent moral chaos and the subsequent educational confusion in the post-war period to the universalism in the aims of education laid down in the Fundamental Law of Education and related documents. Since the beginning of the 1950s various attempts to revert to a more traditional educational philosophy have been made by the conservative government, whose policy has been to re-establish national identity that had been seemingly lost during the Occupation.

As early as 1950 the then Minister of Education, Amano Teiyu, suggested that schools should celebrate national holidays with the rising-sun flag and the national anthem, a practice which reminded the people of the pre-war nationalistic education. He also suggested the setting up for the nation's schools of an ethical code which should act as a substitute for the Imperial Rescript. On the advent of independence in 1952, Prime Minister Yoshida Shigeru stressed the importance of patriotism which was to be cultivated through the proper teaching of national history and geography. His Minister of Education, Okano Kiyotake, immediately referred to the "improvement of social studies, in particular of geography, history, and moral education" to the Curriculum Council, and thus began the revision of the elementary and secondary school curriculum which eventually took place in 1958.

This curriculum revision was the first attempt by the Ministry to make a fundamental change in the school curriculum which had been formulated during the Occupation. The purpose of the revision was stated by the then Minister, Matsunaga Toh, as being "to bring up a nation worthy of true respect and trust in the international community". In order to accomplish this purpose, several measures were proposed, and the first priority was given to strengthening moral education in school by setting aside a minimum of one hour in the weekly timetable for moral instruction. It was expected that a systematic teaching of morals in the school would provide the nation with a common ethical basis.

At the same time, the teaching of national history and geography was to be improved in order to "foster proper understanding and affection for the history, geography, tradition, and culture of our nation". These new directions in moral education and the teaching of history and geography emphasized national identity and clearly indicated a shift in the aim of national education from universalism to particularism or nationalism.

There was another important aspect of the curriculum revision of 1958, which was observed in the measures for "bringing up a nation educated in the new science and technology". The teaching of mathematics and science was to be greatly improved by increasing teaching hours as well as by raising the standard of teaching. Further, the existing vocational subjects in the middle school were to be changed to "industrial arts", through which skills and knowledge necessary for industrial society were to be acquired.

This second aspect of the curriculum revision stemmed from general discontent, as did the first aspect, which had developed by the early 1950s. Partly because of the miserable material conditions surrounding schools in the immediate post-war period, and partly because of the confusion in schools caused by the introduction of the new curriculum, the standard of teaching appeared to many parents to be lowered, an impression that prevailed fairly widely in the society.

The first official criticism was voiced in 1951 by the Advisory Committee for the Revision of the Government Ordinances which examined the policies and Ordinances that had been made during the occupation. With regard to the educational policies, the Committee stated that, while the post-war educational reform contributed to the democratization of the system of education, it was too idealistic and too easy to adopt foreign ideas and practices. First of all, therefore, an attempt should be made to establish a system of education which would be suitable for national conditions, in proportion to national strength, and efficient in the production of necessary and useful human resources to be employed in various circles of society.

This utilitarian approach to education was advocated also by the industrial circle. In 1956, Nihom Keieisha-dantai Renmei (Nikkeiren), an association of the big industrial management concerns, issued a statement "On Technical Education to Meet the Need of the New Era". In the following year the House of Representatives of the National Diet passed a resolution for the improvement of technical education, teaching of science and mathematics, and research in natural sciences. Similar statements and resolutions were made in the same period by the Japanese Academic Council, the Council for Youth, the Council for the Industrial Rationalization, and the Council on Science and Technology. There is no doubt that the curriculum revision of 1958 was made under such a demand of the time.

These new emphases in the aims of education, that is to say, nationalism and utilitarianism, which were most clearly felt in the curriculum revision of 1958, apparently reflected the change of emphasis in the national goal of Japan which had been taking place by the middle of the 1950s. The restoration of national identity was first achieved through Japan's political independence in 1952, and now it was the economic independence that Japan had to strive for in the decade of the 1950s. In entering this new era of higher industrial growth, however, more realistic policies were desired, above all in the field of education. Thus the earlier educational policy of bringing up citizens for a democratic and peaceful nation now looked somewhat too idealistic, and instead of this the utilitarian purpose of education, such as the training of human resources useful for industrial society, was advocated.

The self-confidence of the nation which was first restored by political independence, was now further stimulated by the success in the economic recovery in the 1950s. The nationalism thus developed encouraged the nation to re-examine their national values in culture and tradition which had been undermined by the defeat and the Occupation, and to place a new emphasis upon moral education and the teaching of history and geography in the nation's education.

Japan's unprecedented economic growth in the 1960s only promoted this trend further. In 1960 the curriculum of the high school was revised on the line of the 1958 revision with its nationalistic and utilitarian emphasis. In 1963 the Central Council for Education made recommendations for the improvement of higher education with the intention of reorganizing universities and colleges to meet the demands of industrial society. The Council's recommendations for the improvement of upper secondary education in 1966 attempted to streamline education for youths of 15 to 18 with different abilities and aspirations by providing them with a diversified curriculum, which in turn should satisfy the diversified needs of industrial society.

In the same year, the Central Council issued a document of some 4000 words called "The Image of the Ideal Japanese" which was intended to provide a philosophical background for the proposed reform of upper secondary education by clarifying the moral and ethical qualities of the ideal Japanese. It stated sixteen qualities which were grouped into four subgroups as follows:

I. *As an individual*
   1. To be free.
   2. To develop individuality.
   3. To make much of self.
   4. To possess a strong will.
   5. To possess a sense of awe and respect.

II. *As a member of the family*
   1. To make the home a place of love.
   2. To make the home a place of rest.
   3. To make the home a place of education.
   4. To make the home open.

III. *As a member of society*
   1. To be devoted to work.
   2. To contribute to social welfare.
   3. To be creative.
   4. To show respect for social norms.

IV. *As a national of Japan*
   1. To possess the proper form of patriotism.
   2. To love and respect the symbol of the State.
   3. To foster excellent national characteristics.

The rationale for making this "Image" was explained by Kosaka Masaaki, an eminent philosopher and the Chairman of the Subcommittee of the Council which drafted the statement. According to him, the consensus of the Committee was that the Fundamental Law of Education was abstract in expression and did not fit the particular situation of Japan, although it might well be applicable to any part of the world because of its universal nature. The principles of education were de-nationalized in the Fundamental Law of Education in which, in fact, no single word about Japan or the Japanese was ever mentioned. It was, therefore, necessary to materialize the universalistic principles of the Law in more concrete terms, such as those in the "Image".

Despite their claims to concreteness, the early part of the list does not strike one as being so particularly Japanese, as does the last part "As a national of Japan". With regard to the latter, the commentary states that it is an undeniable fact that the Emperor has long established his unchallengeable position as a symbol of Japan and of the unity of the Japanese people. Therefore respect and affection for the Emperor should lead to respect and affection for the country. Since man contributes to humanity only through his contribution to his country, a proper patriotism is the basis for love of mankind. The Japanese people can contribute to the welfare of mankind by raising the work of the country with their excellent characteristics which have been cultivated and maintained through the history and tradition of Japan.

The "Image" served as an important reference for the Council on Curriculum whose work eventually resulted in the curriculum revisions for elementary schools in 1971 and for middle and high schools in 1972. One of the principles underlying the new revisions was to cultivate the qualities necessary to be a useful member of the State and society, and, as the "Image" suggested, in order to nourish a sense of patriotism, the emphasis was given to promote appreciation of the culture and traditions of the nation through the improvement of teaching, not only in social studies and Moral Education, but in all subjects. At the same time, the revisions attempted to make a further advancement of teaching in science, mathematics, and industrial arts from the utilitarian point of view.

While the government's increasing emphasis on nationalism and utilitarianism in the aims of education has found its supporters among a fairly wide circle of society, there has been equally widely spread criticism against this trend. The opponents agree on the necessity of curriculum reform in accordance with the changes in society, but fear that the government might have gone too far in these directions. The nationalism and utilitarianism in education may have made a great contribution to the unprecedented growth of Japanese wealth in the 1950s and 1960s. As the over-stress in industrialization has been causing various problems in society which are observed typically in the increasing pollution and environmental damage, the over-emphasized utilitarianism in education has produced much educational damage such as, for example, severe competition in university entrance or test-oriented curricula in schools. The nationalism, as advocated by the Central Council, reminds the opposition of the pre-World-War-II nationalistic education, which is certainly unsuitable to the present international age.

The aim of national education is a reflection of the national goals which are conceived by the people. When the people are divided in their views on national goals, it is hard to find a national consensus in the aim of national education as the case of Japan shows.

CHAPTER 4

Control of Education

As observed in the previous chapter, the basic characteristics of the present system of control in Japanese education have been determined by the Constitution of Japan of 1946 and the Fundamental Law of Education of 1947. The Constitution established the principles of democratic government by which the popularly elected National Diet was vested with the power to set up policies relating to various spheres of national life, including education. Once the policies are set, the execution of them is handed to the Executive, the Prime Minister and his Ministers. Of these, the Minister of Education is responsible for national education, but under the principles of democratic government his area of jurisdiction is defined and limited by laws. His executive power is also limited by the principle of local self-government set up by the Constitution in which the local population is given certain powers of self-determination in such matters with which they are directly concerned, such as education.

Following the promulgation of the Fundamental Law in 1947, the Board of Education Law and the Ministry of Education Establishment Law were enacted in 1948 and 1949 respectively. These two laws set up a new pattern of educational administration in which control of education was given directly into the hands of the local population. They should elect a local board of education in each locality by direct vote so as to make education the matter "responsible to the whole people", and to avoid "improper control" from any partisan interests. The central Ministry of Education should remain fundamentally an advisory and assisting body, with the function, as the Fundamental Law of Education specifies, of "establishing conditions required for the pursuit of the aims of education".

This pattern of educational administration has since then been subject to some modifications. In 1956 the Board of Education Law was replaced by a new Law Concerning the Organization and Functions of Local Educational Administration, in which the board members were now to be appointed by the head of the local self-governing body. At the same time, with this new law and other revisions in the Ministry of Education Establishment Law, the Ministry of Education gained certain powers of control over the local boards. This modification was a stepping-stone in the direction of the centralization of power in the control of national education, which has now taken place, and which has met with severe opposition and criticism.

In this chapter the question of controlling national education in Japan will be examined by dealing, firstly, with the machinery for policy formation in national education, secondly, with the systems of educational administration both at the central and local levels, and, finally, with the present dispute which has been caused by the recent trend of centralization of the control of national education.

STRUCTURE FOR THE FORMATION OF NATIONAL POLICIES IN EDUCATION

Education is proclaimed by the Constitution as a right of the people which is to be ensured through the laws enacted by their representatives in the National Diet. The Diet names the Prime Minister and delegates the executive responsibility of the laws to him and his Ministers of whom the Minister of Education is responsible for matters of national education. The National Diet consists of two houses — the House of Representatives and the House of Councillors, and in each there is a Standing Committee on Education in which government policies on education are extensively examined and in which the first step for law-making takes place. Through committee meetings and the plenary sessions of both Houses, the Diet provides a national forum in which both government and opposition views on questions of national education are presented and discussed. The questions cover wide areas of national education — from those relating to the national budget on education to the content of school textbooks. For important issues public hearings are held in which the opinions of the people are directly presented to this national forum.

The seats in the two houses of the National Diet have for some time been shared by the five national parties: the majority conservative Liberal—Democratic Party, the Japanese Socialist Party, the Komei Party, the Japanese Communist Party, and the Democratic Socialist Party. Each party has its own educational policies and its own methods influencing national education.

The present Liberal—Democratic Party and its forerunners have been in power almost continuously since the end of World War II, and therefore have been mainly responsible for the formation and development of the government's policies in national education for the past quarter century. This party represents groups of varied interests, from the big business concerns in the towns and cities to the farmers in the villages, from the nationalistic conservatives to the enlightened liberals, and from higher executives in government and non-government offices to the unorganized workers in small farms. Since the policies of the party reflect such different interests, they are often eclectic and *ad hoc* rather than of a dogmatic nature, but on the whole the party adheres to policies for national stability and prosperity, based on the principles of free enterprise and a welfare state.

In the field of education the policies of the party have followed three main points of emphasis. The first is to regard education as a political tool for national solidarity and stability. National education should first of all nourish the sense of national identity among the young generation. This view is strongly held, especially by the idealogically right wing of the party, which advocates the restoration of some of the traditional nationalistic values in education which could provide the moral basis for national unity. The second emphasis is to make education a means for economic and industrial development. Education would provide a sound basis for economic progress by promoting political stability. It should further train the personnel and manpower which industry would require. This emphasis is a reflection of the interest of the business and industrial circles who support the party.

Thirdly, the party is in favour of strengthening the leadership of the central government in education. Unlike a typical conservative—liberal party, this Liberal—Democratic Party of Japan does not promote the idea of *laissez-faire,* but believes in planning and in central direction, particularly in matters of national education. This is in accord with the tradition of Japanese national education and is easily accepted by the conservative elements of the people. This trend has been particularly promoted by the group of retired civil servants who make up an important element of the party. The centralization of power has also been supported by those representing the business interests who regard it from the viewpoint of business efficiency.

The Socialist Party is the second most powerful political group and has formed a hardcore of anti-government forces except for a short period in 1947—8 when it formed a coalition government with the then second favourite conservative Liberal Party. The socialists depend heavily on organized labour, including a militant Japanese Teachers' Union. The Party in fact includes a large number of teachers union members and acts as a spokesman for the union. The socialists disagree with the liberal—democrats in their educational policies mentioned above, above all in the centralization of power in the government.

The irony of the socialists promoting decentralization and the con-servatives promoting centralization will be explained later in relation to the question of local educational administration. It remains doubtful whether the educational policies of the socialists stem from its Marxist-oriented doctrines or are motivated by its anti-government sentiment. The contribution of the socialists seems so far to be in critical opposition rather than in positive policy innovation. This may be a result of the fact that the Party has been so long out of power. The same might apply to other parties which have been too weak to be effective in formulating national policies of education. The actions of these parties have been motivated mostly by their anti-government stance, although they naturally differ from one another in the degree of their opposition to the govern-ment Liberal—Democratic Party.

These political parties have their own commissions on education which play an important role in the formation of the party policies on education. The policies can be stated in general terms or can be specifically about particular questions, and in any case, through their activities both within and outside the National Diet they have a considerable influence on the policies formulated by the government. This is particularly true in the case of the party in power.

The Education Commission of the Liberal—Democratic Party has some fifty members who meet regularly with the Minister of Education and his senior officials, and who formulate the educational policies of the party. The Commission reflects the somewhat diverse interests within the Party, and consists of individuals with a wide range of backgrounds, but for some time a hard-core of right-wing politicians has taken over the leadership of the Commission and given its policy lines the ideological colour of this group, which has been shown in such questions as moral education, education for patriotism, and teachers' unions.

Besides these political parties, at least three institutions should be mentioned for their influence upon national educational policies and politics. The first one is the judicature, which under the Constitution stands independently from the legislature and the executive. The Supreme Court is granted the power to determine whether a law, order, regulation, or official action is or is not in conformity with the Constitution. The lower courts and the Supreme Court deal with cases of dispute, and their decisions provide judicial precedents which, like the statute laws, have legal force. During the 1960s, the number of court cases in education increased as the conflict between local authorities and teachers' unions was intensified as a result of increasing government control over local schools and teachers. The court cases usually take time, however, and have little direct influence on the immediate execution of government policies.

For example, between 1961 and 1964 the government and teachers' unions fought each other on the issues of the nationwide achievement tests that were conducted by the local education authorities under the direction of the Ministry of Education, and the suits were undertaken at various lower courts. The decisions of the courts were almost equally divided, but most of the decisions which questioned the legality of the tests were made only after 1964 when the Ministry decided on its own initiative to abandon the tests on a nationwide basis and to conduct them only on a sample basis. In the long run, however, the court decisions certainly influence the policies of the government, particularly when the government loses a case.

The teachers' unions are another group which has influence upon national policies in education. The Japanese Teachers' Union (JTU) is a federation of prefectural teachers' unions, each of which negotiates its employment conditions with the prefectural board of education who employs them. As the unions of the teaching profession, they are naturally interested in policy matters on education, and the JTU exercises its leadership in pushing their interest on a national level. The JTU, with some 588,000 members, is affiliated to the General Council of Trade Unions, which supports the socialists and thus constitutes a strong opposition to the government and the government Liberal—Democratic Party. The involvement of the teachers' unions in politics, together with the antagonism of the Liberal—Democrats towards the unions, has caused difficulties in direct communication between the Ministry of Education and the JTU. As a result of this, the JTU has tended to express its view on policy matters through direct appeal to the public or through the opposition parties, above all the socialists.

Another important group which exercises pressure over national policies on education includes associations of industrial and business interests. In general they are in support of the conservative and moderate parties. They exert their influence either through the party machinery or by direct appeal to the government and to the general public. Their activities in national education, particularly in the field of education for industrial development, will be examined in the next chapter.

CENTRAL ADMINISTRATION OF EDUCATION

The laws define the powers of the Ministry of Education. The Ministry of Education Establishment Law specifies that "such powers shall be exercised in accordance with laws" (Article 5) and that "with regard to the exercise of its powers, the Ministry of Education shall not exercise control either administrative or operational, unless otherwise provided for by laws" (Article 5—2). The functions of the Ministry prescribed by the laws are as follows:

Firstly, the Ministry carries out studies and makes plans with regard to measures for the promotion of education in and out of school, higher learning, and culture. Such studies and planning includes the functions and organization of the local education authorities and also includes matters regarding the teaching personnel that the latter employs. The Ministry collects and publishes data for statistical surveys and findings in education, higher learning, and culture. It was under this part of jurisdiction that the Ministry forced the local boards of education to carry out the nation wide achievement tests in 1961—4.

Secondly, the Ministry sets up standards with regard to the physical conditions, personnel, organization, and content of education in the different levels of schools, universities, and other educational institutions. How far the Ministry can make such standards which are enforceable is still a matter of controversy. In general, the Ministry's role in setting up standards of physical conditions, personnel, and organization is accepted by all concerned. With regard to the content of education, however, opinions are divided as to whether or not the Ministry can enforce the standards that it makes. Indeed, the Ministry itself had no positive attitude until 1958, when it introduced new articles into the Enforcement Regulations for the School Education Law by which the curriculum of all elementary, middle, and high schools should be decided in accordance with the standards that the Ministry would make.

Thirdly, the Ministry provides guidance and advice to boards of education, local authorities, universities, and other educational, cultural, and scientific institutions. The Ministry can request them to submit reports and, if necessary in the light of laws and regulations, it can request them to take necessary steps to improve the defaults. The advice is given by means of correspondence, circulars, interviews, and visits of the administrative officers, supervisors, and subject specialists in the respective offices. The Ministry holds conferences and workshops for this purpose. The publication of guides, manuals, and handbooks is another way of advising.

Fourthly, the Ministry assists local boards of education in providing grants-in-aid for such matters as the salaries of teachers in elementary, middle, and special schools, and the cost of educational materials for science teaching and technical education. Such grant-in-aid works in general in such a way that the Ministry pays one-half or one-third of the estimated cost. The Ministry also provides financial assistance to private schools and universities in science and technical education and other limited fields. Most of the government subsidies to the private institutions come from the trust funds established by the government and under the jurisdiction of the Ministry of Education.

Fifthly, the Ministry is given powers to approve certain matters which include the establishment of universities and other educational, scientific, and cultural institutions, the appointment of the superintendents or chief education officers of the boards of education in prefectures and major cities, and textbooks to be used in elementary, middle, and high schools.

Finally, the Ministry establishes and maintains state universities (as of 1970, 75), junior colleges (22), technical colleges (49), and high schools (3 telecommunication, 5 navigation). Also under its jurisdiction come national institutes in educational research, adult education, youth services, statistical mathematics, genetics, Japanese language, an international latitude observatory, and several national museums.

In carrying out such functions the Ministry of Education is equipped with three groups of personnel, each having a different capacity and functioning in a different way. The first group is political, consisting of the Minister of Education and his parliamentary Vice-Minister. The second is a corps of civil servants in the Ministry who assist the Minister with their administrative and technical expertise. The third is a group of experts who serve in the advisory councils or committees of the Ministry.

The Minister of Education is the political head of the Ministry and is himself a member of the Cabinet. However, he does not necessarily have a seat in the National Diet nor is he necessarily a party member. In fact, in the post-war period after 1945, the first eight Ministers of Education, including four who were appointed under the new Constitution, were all recruited from the academic world and had no seat in the Diet. This practice, however, ceased in 1952, and since then all Ministers of Education have been party politicians.*

The change from having a non-partisan Minister to having a political Minister marked a turning point in the policies of the Ministry of Education, which became more directly influenced with politics. The period of non-partisan ministership coincided with the years of post-war educational reform when the initiative for reform came from the Occupation Authority, on the one hand, and from educators, on the other hand, and even the political parties were more or less in general agreement about it. These ministers also brought a group of academicians into the higher rank of the ministerial bureaucracy, and relied heavily on the professional advice of the various councils and committees, notably the Educational Reform Council, which consisted largely of educators and academicians. They were even able to get the co-operation of the teachers' unions, which later became very strongly opposed to the Ministry.

Towards the end of the occupation period, however, the political parties and popular opinion began to disagree about what the educational policies should be after independence. The attempts of the conservative groups to restore national identity through education and to re-examine educational reform in a more realistic light met with strong objections

*In December, 1974, a non-party politician Minister of Education once again turned up when Mr. Nagai Michio, ex-professor of education and the then editorial columnist of the Asahi Newspaper, was appointed to the office.

from the opposition political parties as well as from educators and teachers' unions. It was no coincidence that the first appointment of the politician Minister Okano was made only four months after Japan regained its independence in 1952. His job was to get back the initiative of educational administration from the hands of the academics and educators and to reorientate the educational system under his political initiative on the lines set up by his conservative party. In the following years these were effectively carried out by him and his successors, who were also politicians. This may sound quite normal in a parliamentary system where a political party representing the people takes a lead in forming policies. But in this case these politician Ministers, remaining loyal to the party, mixed education with politics as can be seen clearly in their handling of the teachers.

By that time the teachers, thanks to their unions, had grown up as a strong political power and had exercised considerable influence on national and local politics by backing the opposition Socialist Party. Furthermore, they had succeeded in sending a large number of the union leaders to the local boards of education, and were thus directly confronted by the conservative parties which had also sent to the Board their party members or supporters. Minister Okano's attempt to ban the political activities of teachers by giving public school teachers the status of state civil servants was blocked in the National Diet by very strong opposition both within and outside it. However, his immediate successor, Minister Odachi, formulated the Law Governing Provisional Measures for Securing Political Neutrality of Compulsory Education in 1954, with the purpose of restricting political activities in the public school system. The reform of local education administration of 1956, which will be dealt with in the next section of this chapter, was also mingled with politics under the other ministers in 1954–5. Despite strong opposition in educational circles, it was forcefully carried out by the political majority in the National Diet with the intention of reducing the influence of the teachers' unions in local administration.

The curriculum revision of around 1960, which was most highlighted by the introduction of moral education, can be seen as another example of political influence over education, mention of which has already been made in the previous chapter. In the Ministry's policies of the 1960s, emphasis was given to the improvement of instruction in science and technology. This was due to the increasing demand of industry and business, which wanted to use education as a tool for industrial development and efficiency. The relationship between the business group and the Ministry of Education will be discussed in the next chapter.

The Minister of Education is assisted by the corps of the Civil Service in the Ministry, which is headed by the Permanent Vice-Minister. As of 1971, the internal subdivisions of the Ministry consist of a Minister's Secretariat and five bureaus of Elementary and Secondary Education, Higher Education and Science, Social Education, Physical Education, and Administration.* The Agency for Cultural Affairs is attached to the Ministry, and its internal subdivisions consist of the Commissioner's Secretariat and the Departments of Cultural Affairs and Cultural Properties Protection. The civil servants working in these bureaus consist of two groups — administrative and specialist. The latter include supervisors and subject specialists who are roughly comparable with Her Majesty's Inspectors in England. However, in the case of Japan they do not form a special corps within the Ministry but are spread throughout the bureaus or in various sections of the bureaus, and they work under the directors of the bureaus or the chiefs of the sections who are administrative officers.

Since 1971, there are fourteen councils in the Ministry of Education in addition to four councils in the Agency for Cultural Affairs. Among them the Central Council for Education is concerned with overall policy questions, while others deal with curriculum, science and technical education, health and physical education, teacher training, social (adult) education, university chartering, university problems, private universities, technical colleges, textbook authorization, scientific research, geodesy, selection of persons for cultural honours, Japanese languages, copyright compensation, religious affairs, and cultural properties protection.

The purpose of setting up such councils is to bring as many varying opinions as possible into the formation of the government policies in supplementing party government which inevitably brings a party line into policy making. This is regarded as being particularly important in the field of educational administration which is to be carried for the interest of all

---

*In June 1974 the Bureau of Higher Education and Science was reformed as the Bureau of Higher Education, and a new Bureau of Science and International Affairs was created.

the people. It should also bring expert opinions in to the formation of educational policies.

The Central Council for Education is a successor to the Educational Reform Council which made a great contribution to post-war educational reform during its existence between 1946 and 1951. Its thirty-five recommendations covered all aspects of education and most of them were eventually put into practice through the parliamentary acts and the Ministry's regulation. The role of the Educational Reform Council was to clarify details of educational reform following the general direction of the occupation authority and to make recommendations to the Prime Minister, and therefore the initiative of its work was not exactly in its own hands. None the less, the Council exercised its initiative as well as it could within these limits, and thus the reform was carried out by the Japanese themselves.

In 1951 the Educational Reform Council completed its mission on post-war educational reform, and in 1953 was reorganized into the Central Council for Education. The new Council was to study the matters relating to fundamental policies for education which were referred to it by the Minister of Education, and was to make recommendations to him. During the 1950s the major concern of the Central Council was to improve the national system of education which had been founded basically by the Educational Reform Council, and thus dealt with a wide range of questions such as the enforcement of the extended compulsory education, the improvement of social studies, medical and dental education, the selection of university students, the improvement of education in remote areas, the salaries of teachers, private education, the encouragement of international exchanges in education, science, and culture, assistance to students, and special education.

It also dealt with such problematic issues as the measures to maintain the political neutrality of teachers, the system of school textbooks and teachers' training, all of which caused strong controversy. The Central Council of this decade was also concerned with questions relating to education for industrial development such as technical education and education for working youths.

In the 1960s the Central Council was given the task of examining the existing national system of education and of formulating a plan for reform. It discussed university reform, the improvement of upper secondary education, the image of the ideal Japanese, the immediate measures to meet the student unrest, and guidelines and the master plan for the reform of the school and university system. Its reports raised considerable interest, both favourable and unfavourable.

In the course of development from the Educational Reform Council to the Central Council for Education of the past quarter century, a notable change has been observed in the composition of the membership, which has an important influence on the nature of their work. In the Reform Council the members were almost exclusively educators or those directly related to education. The Reform Council of 1950, for example, headed by the president of Tokyo University, included 12 presidents of universities, 6 university professors, and 7 principals of elementary and secondary schools. Another 8 members, including a representative from the Japanese Teachers' Union, also represented different fields of education. In contrast to the Reform Council, the Central Council for Education has broadened its membership. For example, the Central Council of 1971 included 11 former and present university presidents and professors, 4 school principals, 3 journalists, and 3 leading businessmen. While the presence of leading businessmen might be considered to be an addition, an important omission was the lack of representatives from teachers' or labour unions. This lack was considered by its critics as a weak point in the composition of the membership of the Central Council. Another point of argument was the static quality of the membership; many members had served over several terms, including the Chairman Morito, who had acted as chairman since 1954. The Council was also criticized because of over-representation by the older generation; the average age of the members in 1971 being 67 years.

These points seem to have been considered by the Ministry, and an overall change of membership was made in the Spring of 1972. Accordingly, the members of the new Council are all new, except for three who have continued their term, and include younger individuals (the average age of the new Council members being 56 years). They also include a labour representative besides 2 business men, 5 university presidents and professors, 4 educators and educational administrators, and 4 writers and journalists. The first question that has been referred to them by the Minister of Education is on international exchanges in the fields of education, higher learning, and culture.

LOCAL EDUCATIONAL ADMINISTRATION

The system of boards of education was first introduced in 1948 by the Boards of Education Law, which stated in its first article the objective of the law in the following terms:

"The law aims at attaining the primary objectives of education by establishing boards of education to execute educational administration based on equitable popular will and actual local conditions, with the realization that education should be conducted without submitting to undue control and should be responsible to all the people."

This statement indicated three principles for the new local system of educational administration. Firstly, educational administration should be based on equitable popular will; secondly, it should be adapted to the local conditions; and, thirdly, it should not submit to undue control. These three principles were made on reflection of the pre-war situation in local educational administration, where local education had been uniformly controlled by the central political power.

To realize the three principles the law made provisions to set up in the same year a board of education in each of the forty-six prefectures and in selected cities and towns during 1948, and in the rest of the cities and towns by 1952. The members of these boards of education should be directly elected by the residents of the prefectures or municipalities except for one member who was to be elected among the local diet members. The boards of education thus to be set up consisted of 6 directly elected members and 1 indirectly elected member in the case of prefectural boards and 4 directly elected and 1 indirectly elected in municipal boards. They were to be assisted by a professional superintendent of education and his staff. The board was independent of the general administrative structure, and was responsible for administering education in the area, both in school and out of school. It was given powers to establish and maintain schools and other educational institutions, to make curricula for its own schools, and to appoint personnel for them. It also made its own budget, although this was subject to the approval of the local diet in the area since the board did not have fiscal independence such as is the case in the United States.

The new system was not entirely without problems. First of all, the system was completely new to the Japanese, and it would take time for them to master this system. The first election in 1948 was voted at by only 57 per cent of the electorate, and the second one in 1950 by only 53 per cent. Because of such low interest it was possible for individuals or groups with political ambition to abuse the system of election for the board. Thus despite the alleged neutrality of board members, there were among them individuals who represented various political and professional interests. The overall result of the 1948 election led to conservative domination, but also included a large representation of teachers. Among the total number of prefectural board members, 35 per cent were ex-teachers who constituted the largest single professional group. The fact that many of them were supported by the organized teachers' unions alarmed the conservatives who regarded the unions as their arch-enemy.

When the election for the boards in the prefectures and selected major cities was taking place in 1948, the question still remained as to whether the boards should be set up in all cities, towns, and villages, and this question was to be studied further by an expert committee which eventually made its recommendation in 1951 that the establishment of municipal boards should not be compulsory but should be left to the discretion of each community. Despite the recommendation, which had fairly wide support, a decision was made to make the establishment of boards compulsory. This was done by the strong initiative of the conservative Liberal Party which was then in the government and which expected the new municipal boards to tame the union activities of teachers at the grass-root level. It was generally recognized that the teachers' unions were more radical on the national and prefectural levels, where they could co-operate with other organized labour, and more moderate in the municipalities, particularly in rural areas, where teachers were scattered and tended to be isolated from the major labour movement.

Thus by 1952 a total of 9958 boards of education had been set up in the prefectures and all municipalities, but naturally there was doubt about the quality and efficiency of the administration of many of them. The fragmentation of administration into too small and too many units made the effective management of schools almost impossible. The independence of educational administration from the general administration, which caused the latter much frustration, was another source of difficulty. Where financial resources were limited, as they were in most cases, the conflict between the two administrations became very much greater.

It is fair to say that the new board system provided an invaluable opportunity to teach the people that it was they who should control the schools through the boards they elected. The boards of education in their turn tried to make education the responsibility of the people. Indeed, it can be said that the difficult tasks of post-war reconstruction and reform in education were made possible only by such popularly elected and supported boards. Nevertheless, the problems inherent in the system made it inevitable that there must soon be another reform.

By the middle of the 1950s the reform of the board system had become necessary for two reasons. One was the pressure from the side of the general administration, which had found the independent educational administration to be most inconvenient in an effective and integrated local government. Their frustration seemed to have reached a climax, and the Association of Prefectural Governors repeatedly passed resolutions between 1953 and 1956 demanding the reform of the board system on the grounds that it had become an obstruction to the effectiveness of local administration, that it destroyed unification and comprehensiveness in local government, and that it caused much unnecessary financial strain on local communities. The Association of Municipal Heads expressed the same sentiments.

The other reason for the reform of the board system was a political one. By this time a conflict between the two political elements of the nation, the government conservatives and the opposition led by the socialists, had been brought into the field of education. There was dissatisfaction among the conservative political group who felt that the educational policies of the central conservative government had often been sabotaged by the local boards of education, particularly when these boards were backed by the socialists and other opposition parties and the teachers' unions. Since local general administration was then mostly under conservative majority control, as it was also on the national level, such boards could easily be controlled if they were somehow integrated with the general administration. At the same time, by strengthening central control over local administration, the conservative dominance in local educational administration should be doubly assured. Thus in 1955 an Educational Policy Committee of the conservative Democratic Party proposed three points of reform; the abolition of the municipal boards of education, the appointment of the prefectural boards members by the prefectural governors, and the strengthening of the Ministry's power of control over the boards.

In the following year, 1956, the conservative government presented a bill for the revision of local systems of educational administration to the National Diet with three stated objectives: to secure stability and political neutrality in educational administration, to harmonize educational administration and general administration in local government, and to establish integrated educational administration throughout the state, prefectures, and municipalities. This bill was strongly opposed by the opposition parties, who feared that the democratic principles of local educational administration might be jeopardized by this proposed reform. They were backed by the outside organizations including the National Associations of Prefectural Boards of Education and of Municipal Boards of Education, the Japanese Teachers' Union, and the scholarly Japanese Society for the Study of Education. Twenty-three university presidents and some 600 academicians sent petitions to the National Diet opposing the bill. Despite such opposition both inside and outside the Diet, however, the determined government party passed the bill, which became the Law Concerning the Organization and Functions of Local Educational Administration.

Under the new law, which is now in practice, the members of the boards of education are appointed by the head of the local government with the agreement of the local diet. The term of service is for four years. The number of members is fixed at five in the case of the prefectural board, and at three in the municipal board. The board is assisted by the superintendent who is a local civil servant, and his professional and clerical staff. The office of the board is a part of the executive office of the local government. The board no longer controls its budget for education, but this is under the jurisdiction of the head of the local government. Thus, in contrast to the previous system, the present board of education is an integrated part of the local general administration, and therefore conflict between general administration and educational administration seems to have disappeared. On the other hand, educational administration has lost its independence, and the powers of the board of education have been drastically weakened.

The democratic principle of the people's representation has been retained but with modifications, and the board members are selected not by a direct vote but indirectly through the head of the local government and the local diet, who are both elected by the local people. In order to avoid any partism element on the board, there is a provision which prohibits the appointment of more than one-half of the members of the board from being of a political party. Nevertheless, political neutrality in educational administration has not been guaranteed in the new system any more than in the previous one. There is a danger that the politically elected head and Diet might or might not appoint board members for political reasons. Following the promulgation of the law, the Liberal—Democratic Party issued a circular to its prefectural branches suggesting that they should take measures to exclude from the boards those members who were closely associated with teachers' unions. The then Minister of Education, Kiyose, supporting the Party's actions, stated that the representatives of partisan groups, above all teachers' unions, would not be suitable for membership of the board. These actions already presented themselves as political intervention.

The board of education establishes and maintains schools and other educational and cultural institutions. Prefectural boards usually run high schools and special schools, while municipal boards run middle and elementary schools. The board is responsible for the formulation of a curriculum for its schools in accordance with the course of study set up by the Ministry, and for the adoption of textbooks approved by the Ministry to be used in its schools. The prefectural board issues teachers' certificates and appoints teachers for both prefectural and municipal schools. The prefectural board pays the salaries of these teachers which are, however, partly subsidized by the Ministry.

Although the prefectural board and the municipal boards in the prefecture still remain independent of each other, a hierarchical relationship has been set up between them as seen above with regard to the appointment of teachers. In addition, the prefectural board is given powers to offer advice and assistance to the municipal boards, to require them to submit reports, and, if necessary, to request necessary improvements and corrections concerning their actions. Furthermore, the appointment of the superintendents of the municipal boards requires the approval of the prefectural board.

The same relationship now exists between the Ministry of Education and the prefectural boards. The appointment of prefectural superintendents requires the approval of the Ministry. The Ministry should give advice and assistance to the prefectural and municipal boards and require them to submit reports and request any necessary improvements or corrections. The boards must develop the curriculum of their schools within the guide lines set up by the Ministry.

Thus the integration of educational administration is now assured between central and local educational administration, and in local administration between prefectural and municipal levels. It should improve efficiency of national education in the sense that the different levels of administrative efforts should be better co-ordinated under the leadership and initiative of the Ministry of Education. This is the argument and intention of the successive conservative government parties. The opposition naturally has a different view. It argues that the three principles in the previous board system, i.e. decentralization, direct representation, and independence from general administration have been destroyed by the revision of the system, and that efficiency will now be achieved only at the sacrifice of local initiative and will endanger the democratic principle of educational administration which was established in the Fundamental Law of Education and realized by the previous board of education system.

PROBLEMS IN THE CONTROL OF EDUCATION

The pendulum of educational administration which, as a result of post-war reform, swung from centralization to decentralization, has once more moved back towards centralization. The present system still retains essential elements of decentralization, but in general it is coloured by the tone of centralization. To quote a phrase used by Minister Kiyose, who drafted the present law, there are now clear "lines of command in the educational structure" which go from the Ministry of Education of the central government down to the prefectural board of education and further to the municipal board. At the final end of these lines stand individual schools. Such "lines of command" are set up through various means prescribed by the law and regulations as we have already seen in the previous section. They are further reinforced by such methods as transference of the Ministry's officials to the prefectural boards, each for a term of a few years. There are several cases in which Ministry officials are invited to be prefectural superintendents.

There is currently a great deal of argument on the seemingly increased centralization in educational administration. The proponents of centralization consider it the most suitable form of governing Japan for various reasons. Geographically, Japan is small in size and any region of the country is within easy reach of the centre because of the rapid developments in communication and transportation. The Japanese are a homogeneous nation with a single language and with a single cultural tradition. There are almost no minority racial groups and no religious sectarianism affecting the government. Thus there is no need in Japan for regionalism or decentralization in educational administration, which should cope with the different needs of the localities.

They also argue that as education is a matter of national interest its administration can be most effectively done through the centralized responsibility and power. The central Ministry of Education, with its long-accumulated experiences and prestige, is in a more superior position than any local authorities in handling the questions of national education. In the democratic system of government in which the Ministry is constantly under the control of Parliament, it can well be vested with the responsibility of guaranteeing political neutrality in educational administration both at the central and local levels.

The strongest argument for centralization has come from the fact that Japan has a long history of centralization of government except for a relatively short period of decentralized feudalism which, in the mind of many Japanese, represents a time of chaos. Centralization thus is accepted by them as a natural form of government, the same as the Americans accept decentralization. During the occupation period there was a strong tendency to follow the American pattern of thought and to consider the decentralization of power as the only form of democratic government. The proponents for centralization hold, however, that the direct equation of democracy and decentralization is false. Under the democratic system of government there is a possibility of democratic centralization. Therefore the merits and demerits of centralization of Japanese educational administration should be judged from its actual implications and effects on the realities of Japanese education.

There are, however, genuine concerns about this tendency towards centralization. Above all the opponents of the government's policy doubt if this trend towards centralization is not a politically motivated one and if it does not encourage further political intervention in education. Indeed, there are certain grounds for such doubt. As we observed, the revision of the local educational administration system of 1956 was carried out with a political motive in which the government conservative party hoped to overcome the power of the opposition by strengthening control over the teachers' unions. While admitting the mistakes of the unions, which sometimes mixed education with politics, the Ministry's counter political actions certainly give cause for concern particularly in considering its extended power over the whole area of the nation's education, for which even the militant teachers' unions are no match. It is true that decentralization is no guarantee of political neutrality for education, but the danger of politically controlled centralization may be greater than politically controlled decentralization.

Such concerns are reinforced when the centralization is directed not only at the external conditioning of the educational system but also at the qualitative aspects of education. A series of actions of the Ministry on curriculum revision, including the introduction of moral education and patriotic education, has given rise to a doubt that the Ministry, with its centralized power, is now directing the nation with a particular line of ideology and is interfering with the freedom of thought and belief of the people.

There is a question of interpretation about the definition of educational administration in the Fundamental Law of Education. According to the Ministry the setting up of the standards in curriculum and textbooks is part of their function to "adjust and establish conditions required for the pursuit of the aims of education". Therefore it is perfectly within its prerogative to make necessary revisions in curriculum according to its own best judgement. This interpretation, however, has been questioned by the opposition groups, who consider that the functions of the Ministry under the Fundamental Law are only advisory and assisting, and that the adoption of curriculum should be left to the hands of local authorities and teachers.

In this connection, some consider that the "degenerate morale of classroom teachers" is a result of the tightened central control. The teachers who, under the first board system, had much say in the making of the curriculum and the selection of textbooks, are now under the strict control of the administration in these matters. Thus, instead of exercising their own initiative, they are simply carrying out what they are directed to do, with the inevitable result that their morale is lowered.

The question of central control has been highlighted by the judgement of the Tokyo Court in the 1970 "textbook trial" under Judge Sugimoto in which a suit was brought against the Ministry of Education by Professor Ienaga Saburo of Tokyo University of Education. Professor Ienaga, a professor of Japanese history, had on two occasions in 1962–63 and 1966 been forced to alter the content and expression of his drafts for high school history textbooks under the screening of textbooks by the Ministry of Education. He brought up at the court the question of the legality of the screening system which appeared to him to be clearly against Article 21 of the Constitution on the freedom of expression and publication and Article 10 of the Fundamental Law of Education on educational administration. Thus, starting with the question of the textbook screening system, he touched on the very basic question of educational administration, i.e. who is responsible for the content of education.

The Sugimoto judgement of 1970, which was given to the complaint of Professor Ienaga against the Ministry for the latter's screening of his textbook in 1966, as a whole supported the plaintiff's view. Although it accepted the screening system as legal, the decision ruled that the screening should be applied only to the technical checking and should be done only to ensure that the textbook is up to the general standard: it should not deal with the actual content and thought which the author has the right to express. The decision stated that the right of education is part of the natural right of an individual and it cannot be decided by parliamentary rule.

In other words, the State, however democratically run, has no right to decide what kind of education the people should have. The role of the State is to guarantee the opportunities by which the people will receive the kind of education they wish to have. The teachers, because of their profession entrusted by parents with the education of their children, should be given the freedom to pursue their professional responsibility in teaching, including the selection of textbooks, teaching materials, and the adoption of the methods of instruction. Therefore, the Ministry should neither impose upon teachers the use of particular textbooks, nor make them follow exact details of the Ministry's directives in the school curriculum.

The decision was naturally not welcomed by the Ministry, who held the position that the State was entrusted by parents, through the democratic procedure, with the responsibility of educating children, and that in carrying such responsibility the State should set up standards of education including those of curriculum content, and should screen the textbooks in accordance with these standards. Such measures were necessary to ensure that the children would receive a proper education, which could not be guaranteed if it were left to individual teachers and the authors of the textbooks.

The case is still in the court, as the Ministry immediately appealed to the higher courts, and therefore the final judicial decision is still awaited. Nevertheless, the decision is significant as the first legal opinion which criticized the tendency of centralization, although what effect the decision will have in the future course of Japanese educational administration is still to be seen.*

*In July 1974 the Tokyo Court under Judge Takatsu passed judgement on another case which Professor Ienaga brought against the State for the latter's screening of his textbook in 1962–3. This time the case was decided in favour of the defendent, whose textbook screening system was found constitutional. The issue on the textbook screening, however, is now more complicated by this judgement, which clearly stands in opposition to the previous Sugimoto case in 1970.

CHAPTER 5

Education and Economic Development

Japan's economic progress in the past quarter century is one of the most remarkable phenomena of the modern history of the world. It came out of World War II totally defeated with its territory cut down to nearly half, its overcrowded population left in despair and hunger, its economic life paralysed, and its industrial capacity at an end. Industrial production went down to one-tenth of the 1935–7 level. Yet in scarcely ten years production had already recovered to the pre-war level, and in 1956 the government proudly declared in its white paper on economics that the post-war period of recovery was over and the new era of high rate economic growth had begun. In 1959 the annual rate of economic growth reached as high as 18·3 per cent and kept well above 10 per cent throughout the whole period of the 1960s. Comparatively speaking, in 1958 Japan was ninth in the world with its gross national product. By 1962 it had surpassed India, Canada, and China, and had become the sixth. After a further two years it had passed France and in another year, the United Kingdom. In 1968 Japan overtook West Germany and became the third, with only the United States and the USSR ahead. By the end of the 1960s Japan distinguished itself in many areas of industrial production. It ranked third in the world in electric power generated, crude steel, cars, sulphuric acid, pulp, and cement, second in the world in chemical textiles and plastic goods, and top in steel vessels, trucks and buses, cameras, and radio and television receivers.

This rapid reemergence of Japan as in industrial power has naturally drawn attention both from inside and from outside Japan, and serious attempts have been made to answer the question Why has Japan's economy achieved such swift recovery and growth? Of course it is impossible to find a single answer to this: various factors and conditions

88

have jointly and inter-connectedly contributed. It is not our immediate concern to discuss these causes, and it may be sufficient to note here that, despite a variety of attempted answers, everyone agrees on one point: that the high level of the nation's education contributed a great deal to the high rate of Japanese economic growth.

For example, the 1956 Report of the Organization for Economic Co-operation and Development (OECD), *Economic Surveys: Japan,* stated that the rapid growth of the Japanese economy between 1953 and 1962 was partly due to the high quality of the Japanese workers, products of the national system of education under which by 1958, the report stated, 45 per cent of those youths who had completed nine years compulsory education, continued their education in high schools and 10 per cent of the age groups 18–22 received education in universities or colleges.

It is interesting to see how the Japanese economy and education have made great progress hand in hand in the post-World-War-II period. As Chart III (Appendix) shows, the increase in the gross national product is almost on a par with that of public expenditure in education. During the same period, education, as indicated in the chart by the number of pupils and students receiving secondary and higher education, steadily increased.

It is not easy to establish any causal relationship between these economic and educational phenomena, although the recent development of the "economics of education" has thrown much light on it. However, without the help of positive evidence, which might be produced by a systematic study such as above mentioned, a speculative interpretation may be possible from this chart: that is to say, in the immediate post-war period the existing relatively high level of education assisted the rapid recovery of economics, and after 1955, and particularly after 1960, economic expansion contributed to the expansion of education, which in turn helped a further growth of economics.

In the following sections of this chapter an attempt will be made to analyse this interdependent relationship between education and economic development in Japan through the observation, firstly, of the government's planning of education and economic development, secondly, of the government's policies on technical education, and, finally, of the effects of such planning and policies upon Japanese education at large.

PLANNING IN EDUCATION AND ECONOMIC DEVELOPMENT

The period between 1945 and 1951 was marked as an era of democratization in the Japanese educational system, and the educational policy-makers were preoccupied above all with the broadening of educational opportunities, both in and outside schools, for the training of citizens in political responsibility and their upbringing in general culture. Curiously enough, despite the economic difficulties of the time, little attention was given to education for the economic growth or recovery of the nation. One of the main reasons for this was the uncertainty of the economic future of occupied Japan, and therefore it was only towards the end of the occupation, when the Japanese were allowed to prepare for their own economic future, that proper attention was given to technical education and other fields of education relevant to economic development. In June 1951, a month after independence, the Industrial Education Promotion Law passed the National Diet. The purpose of the Law was stated as follows:

> "In view of the fact that industrial education is the basis of the development of the industry and economy of our country, as well as the improvement of the livelihood of the people, this law . . . . shall aim at promoting vocational education in order to nurse a just and proper belief among the people toward labour, give them practical knowledge concerning industry, and develop their ability to design and create, so that they can contribute to the independence of the economy of our nation."

Under the Law, industrial education councils were to be established both on the national and local levels, and were to deliberate measures for promoting industrial education by setting up comprehensive plans for it, by improving the contents and methods of teaching in the subjects related to it, by securing necessary material conditions, by planning the training of teachers, and by promoting co-operation with industry. The State was to provide for subsidies to local authorities with regard to the equipment and facilities for the teaching of industrial education in middle and high schools, and for the training of teachers for industrial education in universities.

In 1953 the Science Education Promotion Law was promulgated with the intention of promoting science teaching in elementary, middle, and high schools.

These measures were certainly stimulated by the interest of the industrial and business circle, who began to appreciate the importance of education in economic development. In 1952 Nihon Keieisha-dantai Renmei (Nikkeiren), a federation of the big industrial management concerns, issued its first public document on educational policy, "Demand for Re-examining the New Educational System", which bluntly expressed the dissatisfaction of the industrial circle with the democratization-oriented new school system and suggested diversification of high school curricula by introducing more vocational courses and a higher degree of professionalization at the university level of education in accordance with the needs of industry.

Nikkeiren continued to publish views of a similar kind on education in the following years. In 1956 it issued another important statement "On Technical Education to Meet the Needs of the New Era", which was inspired by its keen awareness of industrial competition among the big industrial powers of the world. Referring to the training schemes of scientific and technical personnel in the USSR, the United Kingdom, and the United States, it suggested the setting up of a comparable plan for scientific and technical education in Japan. The plan should aim at (a) promoting scientific and vocational education in elementary and middle schools, (b) improving technical training for working youths, (c) strengthening technical high schools, and (d) reforming higher education in science and technology.

With regard to the last point it was suggested that technical colleges be established which should give intensive technical training for five years after middle school, to encourage the expansion of science and technology faculties in universities by means of state subsidies, to strengthen postgraduate programmes in science and technology, to improve the quality of teaching, and to assure co-operation between industry and academics in scientific and technological education. This statement made a great impression upon government policy, and most of the recommendations were subsequently put into practice.

In 1957 the Economic Planning Agency, which had been set up in 1955 to co-ordinate policies of various departments of the government with regard to long-range economic planning, formulated a New Long Range Economic Plan. It set up guidelines for economic development for the five-year period at a time when the Japanese economy was about to enter a new period of high-rate growth. This plan was the first government economic plan in which attention was duly given to education as a necessary prerequisite of economic growth. In setting up a five-year plan for economic development, it estimated that by 1962 some 27,500 science and technology graduates would be needed annually.

In responding to this economic plan, in 1957 the Ministry of Education referred the deliberation on the measures for promoting scientific and technical education to its Central Council for Education. The latter promptly made recommendations which led the Ministry to formulate in the same year a five-year plan for expanding the number of science and technology graduates by 8000 to make up the estimated shortage by the end of a five-year period beginning 1957.

In 1960 the government, under the economic-minded Premier Ikeda Hayato, adopted a famous National Income Doubling Plan which was intended, as the title suggests, to double the national income in ten years with an estimated rate of 7 per cent annual economic growth. Though it seemed too ambitious, the plan encouraged the industrial and economic potential of the Japanese nation, which was about to explode having passed through the period of economic recovery and preparation for further progress. As it happened, the actual growth surpassed the plan; the annual rate of growth reached an average of 11 per cent between 1961 and 1969, and the planned objective in the gross national product was already achieved in five years. The plan thus had to be modified by the subsequent economic plans of 1965 and 1967, and the GNP of 1969 amounted to 3·7 that of 1960.

The National Income Doubling Plan included an educational plan as an integral part. The Economic Council of the Economic Planning Agency, which drafted the Plan, appointed at the outset of deliberation a subcommittee on education and training among its eighteen subcommittees. The position of the Economic Council on the matter of education was clear in the statement on one of its five planning objectives, "improving human capabilities and encouraging education in science and technology", which expressed:

"In view of the swift progress of science and technology of the increasing complexity of industrial structure, and of the future trend in the labour force, the need has arisen to take up the problems on education, training, and research, in relation to economic growth. These problems are concerned with development of human capabilities and have been hitherto separated from economic questions. Future progress in economics and social welfare depends largely on the effective use of the human resources of the nation".

The subcommittee on education and training of the Economic Council considered that secondary education was a crucial factor in developing the human capabilities of the nation, and suggested that eventually a long-range plan for the improvement of secondary education should be formulated. However, to meet immediate needs during the ten-year period of this economic planning, the subcommittee gave priority to education in science and technology, pointing out that a large number of scientists and engineers of high quality should be provided so that the economic plan would not be handicapped by the default of human resources, and suggesting the setting up of an immediate plan for the improvement of training schemes for scientists and engineers.

The realization of the subcommittee's recommendation on secondary education had to wait until 1963, when the then Minister of Education, Araki, referred the matter to the Central Council for Education for its deliberation. The latter's report, "On the Expansion and Development of Upper Secondary Education", which was eventually submitted to the Minister in 1966, had an important effect upon the course of the nation's secondary education, including technical education on the secondary level, by advocating the reorganization of the latter stage of secondary education on the principle of what is called "diversification of secondary education".

With regard to the recommendation on the training of scientists and engineers, a more elaborate plan was developed by the Council on Science and Technology of the Prime Minister's Office which in November 1960 submitted a report entitled "Science and Technology after Ten Years". The plan specified the levels which should be achieved in ten years in various fields of science and technology to cope with social and economic needs. Measures to encourage activities in research and development were recommended which included the increase of investment in research and development from the rate of 1 per cent of the national income in 1958 to 2 per cent in 1970, the expansion of scientific and technological information systems, and both the quantitative and qualitative improvement of the training of scientific and technical personnel.

On the latter point, the report estimated that in ten years the shortage of science and technology graduates and technical high school graduates would be 170,000 and 439,000 respectively, and suggested the planned expansion of places in the university faculties concerned and in technical high schools. Along with the quantitative expansion, various points of qualitative improvement were suggested in the areas of curricula, teaching methods, teaching staff, and facilities in both graduate and undergraduate programmes in universities and in both general and technical high schools. It also recommended the new establishment of technical colleges in which the training would be somewhere between the level of university and that of high school. The recommendations were put into effect by the Ministry of Education in its 1961 plan to increase the number of places in science and technology faculties from the then existing 28,000 to 44,000 in seven years. As part of this plan of expansion, nineteen new technical colleges with some 2000 places were founded in 1962.

In 1963 the Central Council for Education submitted its report, "On the Improvement of Higher Education", which aimed at the setting up of policy guidelines concerning the objectives, organization, and administration of higher education in order to meet the changing needs of higher education that had been caused partly by its foreseen quantitative expansion, not only in the fields of science and technology but also in other areas. In advocating the "diversification of higher education" the report exercised influence upon the structure of technical education on the higher level, as we shall see later.

Meanwhile, the economic planners continued their work, and the subcommittee responsible for manpower policies of the Economic Council formulated in 1963 its report of "Objectives and Countermeasures for Developing Human Capabilities". This document was worthy of note as a candid statement by the economic planners of their view of education. It contained a few important ideas and suggestions which exerted influence upon the educational policies of the time. Firstly, it advocated a meritocratic idea, suggesting a widely diversified educational system in accordance with the ability level of individuals, as well as the social demands. In such an educational system middle schools were expected to play their role, particularly through their career-guidance service, in selecting youths in accordance with their ability, aptitude, and future career, and placing them in the education routes which should fit the need of the individual as well as of society. High schools should diversify the curricula both in general and vocational education. In order to match the changing structure in industry, the curricula of technical high schools in particular should be expanded and improved. To fulfil the role of training capable leaders and professionals for an industrial society, higher education should be improved both qualitatively and quantitatively. Above all, the programmes for science and technology should be expanded. Junior colleges and technical colleges should be encouraged to expand for the training of middle-rank technicians.

Secondly, the report emphasized the need for the improvement of industrial education for the training of skilled workers both in public institutions and in individual firms. It also suggested that such training for youths between the ages of 15 and 18 might be integrated within the broadly conceived upper secondary education. The necessity of retraining older workers was also considered.

Thirdly, the Manpower Policies Committee advanced the idea of "education as an investment", suggesting an appreciation of the effect of education on the quality of the labour force and thus on industrial progress. In considering the long-range effect of education on the quality of the labour force and thus on industrial progress, it suggested considering education as a necessary investment for industrial growth. It recommended in particular the increase of public and private expenditure in higher education and in industrial training.

As we shall see later, these ideas and recommendations of the economic planners exerted a considerable influence upon the educational policy planners, and became points of issue in the educational politics of the 1960s. Meanwhile two economic plans were made in 1965 and 1967 to adjust the National Income Doubling Plan of 1960, but no new idea on education was developed by economic planners. It was only in the New Economic and Social Development Plan of 1970 that a slightly modified view of education was presented. We shall see it in the last part of this chapter.

EDUCATION FOR ECONOMIC DEVELOPMENT – TECHNICAL EDUCATION IN THE 1960s

Stimulated by the energetic activities of economic planners as well as those of educational planners in the early 1960s, the decade marked a period of great expansion in education, particularly in technical education. The quantitative expansion of technical education in the 1960s is shown in Table 1.

Table 1

	Numbers of students			
	1960	1965	1970	1972
Graduate training	1,537	4,457	12,607	14,476
Undergraduate training	81,684	158,006	283,674	308,322
Junior colleges	8,166	14,203	21,799	22,266
Technical colleges	3,375[1]	22,208	44,314	47,853
Technical high schools	305,687	565,270	565,508	541,412

[1] In 1962 the year of establishment of technical colleges.

A system of technical education consists of several different levels: on top, the faculties of science and technology provide both graduate and undergraduate training; then two-year junior colleges and five-year technical colleges train middle-rank technicians, and technical high schools or the technical courses in high schools produce lower-level technicians. In addition, middle schools give some technical education in their general education curricula. Outside these regular schools there are a large number of institutions both inside and outside industry in which some sorts of technical education are given on various levels. We will discuss schools and universities further in a later chapter and only mention them here in relation to technical education.

Universities train scientists, high-rank technicians, and technologists in their faculties of science, engineering, and agriculture. The undergraduate courses extend for four years, consisting of one and a half years general education and the rest for specialized education, while graduate courses require two years for the Master degree and another three years for the Doctorate. The government's policy indicated in the 1963 report of the Central Council for Education, "on the Improvement of Higher Education", was to concentrate advanced graduate work for technologists in a selected number of universities, while leaving more practical training for high-level technicians in others. The junior colleges with two, or some-times three-year courses, have become less popular among the industrial circle because of the short duration of the courses, and thus, since 1962 they have been somewhat overshadowed by the newly established technical colleges. The latter's courses extend over five years, taking students immediately from middle schools and providing more concentrated practical training for middle-level technicians.

The technical high schools or technical courses of comprehensive high schools train the lower level of technicians. The courses extend over three years for day students and four years for part-time students, and include both general and specialized subjects. A noteworthy tendency in technical high school curricula in the 1960s was an increase in the degree of specialization which was intended to meet the varying needs of industry as well as of students. This trend was initiated in the beginning of the decade by the Ministry of Education through its revision of high school curricula in 1960. The newly revised Course of Study for High Schools stressed the necessity of providing students for appropriate education in accordance with their abilities, aptitudes, and future careers, while it expanded and improved the content of curricula to meet the changing need of industrial society. With regard to technical courses, the revised Course of Study increased the requirement in specialized education and offered wider areas of specialization. It listed 156 technical subjects which, when variously combined, made up seventeen technical courses.*

The Central Council for Education also contributed to this trend in its 1966 report on secondary education. It advocated "diversification of secondary education", which meant, on the one hand, the diversification of high school curricula into various specializations in order to meet the varied needs of students as well as of industrial society, and, on the other hand, the inclusion in high school education of various forms of education which had not been hitherto regarded as proper secondary education. An illustration of the latter was the inclusion of industrial training in secondary education, and we shall be returning to this later.

Pupils in middle schools learn the elements of modern techniques in a subject called industrial art — home-making, as part of their general education. Until 1962 the subject was called vocation — home-making,

*These seventeen included mechanics, automobile mechanics, ship building, electricity, electronics, architecture, civil engineering, industrial chemistry, chemical industry, ceramics, chemical dyeing, spinning and weaving, mining, metallurgy, metalworking, industrial arts, and industrial design. In 1970 five new courses were added: information engineering, industrial measurement, environmental engineering, industrial management, and system engineering.

implying the giving of vocational orientation and orientation for home life to those pupils completing their compulsory education, the majority of whom left immediately for industry or other vocational fields. As the number of those moving to high schools increased during the 1960s however, the need for vocational orientation was felt to have decreased and to be limited only to the minority of pupils. Under the 1962 system the need of this minority was to be met by an independent vocational subject, agriculture, industry, commerce, fishery, or home making, which was offered as a choice. The reason why the subject industrial arts — home-making is an obligatory subject, is to provide pupils with basic technical skills and the understanding of modern techniques as a part of their general education towards life in a modern industrial society. The content of the subject includes drawing, metal and woodwork, mechanics, electronics, and agricultural cultivation. For girls, emphasis is given to the understanding of electrical and other home apparatuses, as well as to cooking, dressmaking, and nursing.

Outside the regular school system there are also various forms of technical training. A large number of young people and adults receive some kind of technical training in the institutions which are classified by the Ministry of Education "miscellaneous schools". In 1969, out of some 1,414,000 persons attending 8000 such schools, some 12 per cent received technical training in such areas as industrial arts, automobile mechanics and electric and electronic mechanics.

From an industrial point of view, more important training is given within or in relation to industry. This training is regulated under the Industrial Training Law of 1958 which was further modified in 1969. Under the Law, training centres are to be set up either by the public authorities or by private firms for the training of skilled workers. The courses of training vary in duration from six months to three years, and in content, which, however, usually includes both basic academic and specialized subjects with a great emphasis on practical work. In 1969, 419 public training centres trained 123,780 workers in their 2317 courses, while in the same year 459 individual firms and 721 co-operatives trained some 83,000 workers in their training centres, 69 per cent of which happened to be youths under the age of 18.

Since the latter part of the 1950s an attempt has been made to bring the industrial training of young people within industry closer to technical high school education. This movement was particularly encouraged by the revision of the School Education Law in 1961, which provided for the recognition, under certain circumstances, of the training in industrial centres as part of the high school graduation requirement. This integration of industrial training and high school education was encouraged by industrial circles who began to realize the need for a higher level of general specialized education for their skilled workers. The training scheme in the training centres in fact became increasingly similar to that of the technical high schools in the 1950s as the former increased the proportion of general or basic education in such subjects as mathematics, sciences, languages, and so on. Yet being out of the regular school system, the trainees in the centres were handicapped in the qualifications they gained when compared with those of high-school students. Consequently, quite a number of trainees also took part-time or evening courses in high schools, but such a course often became a burden on them as well as on their employers, and there was a high drop-out rate among them.

Thus the integration of industrial training and high school education was thought to be beneficial for both employers and employees. For the former's part, particularly, it was considered a wise labour policy to encourage young workers to stay in the same firms by allowing them an opportunity to complete high school education while in industrial training, and some firms had already set up technical high schools either independently or jointly for their own industrial trainees. After the revision of the School Education Law in 1961, more experimental forms developed in which part of the technical high school was given in industrial training centres and the rest in technical high schools.

Kanagawa Prefecture, for example, has developed a system in which part-time technical high schools in co-operation with public training centres offer four-year courses consisting of one year of full-time day education and three years of part-time education on three evenings, or one full day plus one evening per week. The students or trainees receive certificates at the end of the first year stating that they have completed a training-centre course, and at the end of an additional three years they receive a high school diploma. The Takaoka Industrial High School of Toyama Prefecture provides a four-year course which combines one full day and three evenings a week attendance at school, with the frequent visits of specialist teachers to the firms for on-the-job training in practical subjects. By 1970 the Ministry of Education had recognized eighty-six public and private industrial training centres which were to co-operate with neighbouring technical high schools in offering the high school diploma to their trainees.

EDUCATION AND ECONOMIC DEVELOPMENT

To sum up the preceding sections, Japanese technical education, stimulated by successive educational and economic planning, underwent an unprecedented expansion both quantitatively and qualitatively. Not only did the numbers of institutions and students enrolled increase, but also the level and content of the education offered were to a great extent improved and diversified. There is little doubt, as many qualified observers seem to agree, that such an effort to improve technical education in the 1960s rendered a great service to the Japanese economic progress of the time. Of course technical education was not the sole contributor to this, and other areas of education, particularly general education of primary and secondary levels, should also be taken into account. After all, technical education is a part of the whole system of education, and without a sound general education in basic schooling, for example, it would not have been as effective as it was. Furthermore, the economic progress of Japan depended on various conditions, many of which, such as skills at a high level in management, human relations, information, communication, and distribution, to quote a few examples, were products of general education as well as specialized subjects in non-technical fields. We shall come to this point in a later chapter, and here it is necessary only to take note of the contribution of non-technical education to economic progress.

The contribution was reciprocal: as educational development contributed to economic growth, so the latter did to the former. There was an educational expansion both in public expenditure in education and in the percentage of students enrolled in upper secondary schools and universities. Such expansion was clearly due to the economic growth which made it possible for the nation to afford such a level of educational development. The contribution of economic growth was, however, not limited to providing the material conditions for educational expansion, but went further and had a profound effect upon the quality of education. The latter can best be illustrated by the two educational issues which occurred during the 1960s concerning "diversification by ability" and "education as an investment".

As we have seen earlier, the idea of diversifying curricula by ability and aptitude was first advocated by the economic planners in the Manpower Policies Committee of the Economic Council in 1963, which was soon echoed in a similar tone by the 1966 report of the Central Council for Education on upper secondary education. The latter recommended that the opportunities for upper secondary education should be extended through schools and other educational institutions to all young people aged 15—18 to enable them to develop their capabilities to the fullest extent, and they also recommended that the content and form of secondary education should be diversified to meet the needs of society as well as of individuals, varying according to their abilities, aptitudes, future careers, and local conditions. The details of the recommendations will be discussed in a later chapter, but it should be noted that the report suggested among other things the diversification of high school curricula, the improvement of high school education for working youths, and the strengthening of the guidance service in middle schools, all of which had been suggested in the 1963 report of the Manpower Policies Committee of the Economic Council.

The Central Council's report on upper secondary education caused a heated controversy, and one of the reasons for the criticism lay in this "diversification by ability". As we have quoted earlier, the Council did, in fact, advocate the diversification not only by ability, but also by aptitude, future career, and local conditions, but, nevertheless, the general impression was that the Council's real emphasis was on ability. This was unfortunate, because the error in making intelligence the sole criterion for selection was pointed out strongly in the report of the subcommittee which served as a basis for the final report of the Council. The latter, however, made this point less emphatically, and it was overshadowed by such recommendations as special education for high intellectual talent, a recommendation which was apparently motivated by the interest in intellectual ability.

What made matters more complicated was another general impression that the Council's report paid too much attention to industry's interest in economic growth. Because of the resemblance between the Council's report and the 1963 report of the Manpower Policies Committee of the

Economic Council, such an impression was hard to dismiss despite a denial on the part of the Council. In consequence, the opponents interpreted this as meaning that the Central Council for Education advocated the kind of ability which would be useful only for industrial development.

The question of diversifying curricula by ability could have been seen from a more educational point of view. After all, at the stage of mass secondary education which Japan had reached it would be inevitable to diversify the curricula or courses in accordance with the students' abilities. However, the issue became very mingled with politics between opposing factions. The same problem occurred around another controversial issue on "education as an investment", in which the intention to make use of education for economic development was much more evident than in the case of "diversification by ability".

The idea of "education as an investment" was by no means a novel one in the history of Japanese education as we have already observed in the historical chapters. The educational policy planners as well as the general public had long regarded education as a kind of investment which should ensure an individual better social status later in his life. "Learning is the key to success in life", said the Preamble to the Fundamental Code of Education in 1872, encouraging the populace to send their children to school. This was on the individual level, and on the national level also the idea had long been officially accepted as well as exemplified by the continuous endeavour of the government to educate for "national wealth and strength". However, it had been conceived in rather general terms, and no attempt had been made to materialize the idea into a concrete plan until the early 1960s when the educational policy planners first learnt from the economic planners how to express it in educational planning. It took shape in the 1962 White Paper on Education compiled by the Ministry of Education.

As the title *Japan's Growth and Education: Educational Development in Relation to Socio-economic Growth* shows, this White Paper was intended to demonstrate the contribution of education to the economic development of the nation by describing the historical progress of Japanese education over the past ninety years with special reference to the economic development of the nation. It was a timely publication, since 1962 happened to be the ninetieth anniversary of the inauguration of the national system of Japanese education and it was also the year of the economic boom in Japan.

The White Paper consisted of an introductory theoretical chapter on the contribution of education to economic growth, three historical analytical chapters dealing with the spread of education and socio-economic development, and aims and content of education and socio-economic development, and the measures of national effort and distribution of educational investment respectively, and a final chapter on suggested long-term overall educational planning.

The idea of "education as an investment" was developed in the first theoretical chapter. In examining the contribution of education to economic growth, the paper used four indicators: national income, labour force, physical capital, and educational capital. The estimate of educational capital was based on the accumulation of yearly educational expenditure of the national and local government in the public sector, and of yearly private school expenditure. In comparing the growth of these indicators during the period between 1905 and 1960, it was revealed that the labour force and physical capital had grown at the rate of 1·7 times and seven times respectively, while national income had increased almost ten times, thus well exceeding the rates of increase in the other two indicators.

An explanation of this fact given in the White Paper attributed a large part of the growth in national income to the increase of educational capital, which had grown during the same period at the rate of some twenty-three times. In other words, the White Paper tried to explain the fact that the rate of increase in the national income exceeded that in the labour force and in physical capital by adding a new factor – that of "educational capital".

The White Paper further attempted to calculate the return from education which was estimated as the proportion of the total increase in the national income contributed by education. Applying the methods developed by Theodore Schultz of Chicago, who estimated that the contribution of education to the increase in national income in the United States was 33 per cent, the White Paper estimated that the rate in Japan during the period between 1930 and 1955 was 25 per cent.

However, the above calculation was based on several assumptions still to be tested, and thus should not be regarded as positively determined. Nevertheless, it seemed successful in showing how vital for economic growth was the investment in education. It certainly provided the educational policy makers with a tool for persuading their colleagues in other departments, notably that of finance, of the importance of expanding expenditure in education. It also drew the attention of educators and the general public to the fact that education was after all concerned not only with the welfare of individuals but also with the economic success of the nation. Thus the phrase "education as an investment" became for a time a popular catch-phrase among educational policy planners and certain groups of educators.

On the other hand, there were certain misgivings among different groups of educators about the idea of "education as an investment". Apart from a general tendency among educators to be suspicious about any mode of thinking that seemed to give education a secondary role subservient to that of other social functions, they were genuinely concerned about the status of education in such a mode of thinking. They were afraid that this utilitarian view of education implicit in the idea was too narrow and one-sided, and that it would encourage one to judge the effects of education solely by its contribution to industrial efficiency.

To them the idea seemed to take too much notice of the interests of industry and to make education simply a tool for economic growth. After all, education was concerned with the well-being of individuals as well as of society, and "human capabilities for industrial need" should constitute only part of larger aspects of human development. Here the criticism of "education as an investment" merged with that of "diversification by ability", and, in fact, the opponents of these two ideas regarded them as stemming from a single character of the government's policy which seemed to subordinate everything to the interest of industry.

It is interesting to note that even some of the educational policy planners expressed certain reservations about the wholehearted acceptance of the idea "education as an investment". Chairman Morito of the Central Council for Education stated immediately after the 1962 White Paper appeared that it was an important new way of thinking to consider education as the development of human capabilities and to regard the cost of education as a productive investment in human resources, but it was doubtful whether human development as an objective of education could be achieved by the development of only those capabilities which educational investment looked for.

"Image of the Ideal Japanese", a report of the Central Council for Education which was published at the same time as the 1966 report on upper secondary education, stated that the industrial growth of Japan would require not only the development of human capabilities but also the improvement of human qualities, without which human beings would degenerate into just the means for industrial processes. It went on further to say that the ideal of a welfare state could be materialized not only by material wealth produced by the development of human capabilities, but also by the high moral standards of the people created by the improvement of human qualities.

The point expressed by the "Image" seemed to gain some ground in the late 1960s both in economic and educational planning, which began to appreciate the need for education towards human quality in addition to its continued interest in education for industrial development. In the field of economic planning this new concern developed while the Economic Council deliberated over their two plans, the Economic and Social Development Plan of 1967 and the New Economic and Social Development Plan of 1970. By that time it had become a matter of wider knowledge that, while the Japanese economy had been brought to an unprecedented degree of prosperity by its high rate growth policy, it had to face new problems which were partly the result of this policy. For one thing, the progress had been made mostly in heavy industrial sectors, leaving behind many other economic and social sectors, such as agriculture, small and medium-sized enterprises, consumer price control, housing, and various areas of social welfare. Therefore, the objective of these economic and social development plans was to develop "economy and society on balanced and solid bases" by integrating economic growth and social welfare.

With regard to education, the first report, which was published in 1967, continued the traditional preoccupation of economic planners with education for science and technology, but the second in 1970 extended their interest further, and considered education as a foundation for the balanced development of economics and society. It proposed several measures for the improvement of education after examining the demands made upon it by an industrial society. As expected, first priority was given to the improvement of science and technical education both in and out of the school system, but after this its recommendations dealt with non-technical aspects of education. It suggested the improvement of education by cultivating necessary qualities to aid international co-operation. This was to cope with the increasing internationalization of economic activities in which the teaching of certain new knowledge, skills, and insight was urgently required.

Out-of-school education received special attention from the plan as an important means of re-educating the adult population for their re-adjustment to a rapidly changing society. This out-of-school education should be restructured, particularly in the light of the new concept of life-long education. A reduction in the number of working hours would increase the importance of education for leisure, which would be aimed at cultivating various forms of human activities, such as art, music, sport, etc. Finally, the plan stressed that it was necessary in education to keep an even balance between the sciences and humanities in order to produce well-integrated individuals who could cope with such a changing society.

This new emphasis placed on non-technical education by the economic planners in the last part of the 1960s probably indicated the beginning of a new relationship between education and economics in which education was to contribute to economic development not only through its direct attention to industrial interest in science and technical education, but also through its proper concern with human qualities in general. This question had been discussed by the Central Council for Education in its 1967 report on the "Images of the Ideal Japanese" and in more concrete terms in its "Fundamental Measures for Educational Reform", which was published in 1971 as a result of its four-year deliberations. We shall come back to this report in the last chapter.

CHAPTER 6

School and Society

"ZEAL FOR EDUCATION"

"This ongoing educational revolution is due above all to the 'zeal for education' of the people", commented a well-informed observer of the progress of Japanese education in the 1960s. When he made this remark, however, he only repeated an opinion which had been generally voiced by many other observers. It is true, as we have already noted in the earlier chapters, that the progress of Japanese education has owed much to the initiative of the government as well as to the concern of industry. Their efforts, however, would not have produced the results we now see without the support of the people at large. On the other hand, it is this "zeal" or "over-zeal" for education which has been blamed by many equally well-informed observers as the cause of the evils in Japanese education, such as the severe competitive examination system and various pathological phenomena including cases of "schoolphobia" among schoolchildren and suicide cases among young people.

In this chapter an attempt will be made to examine the nature of this "zeal for education" or the attitudes toward education of the Japanese people and to analyse some of its effects upon the policies and practices in Japanese education which are most typically revealed in the problems related to admission to universities and high schools.

One of the methods used in assessing popular attitudes toward certain social issues is the opinion survey which has been widely used during the past decades in Japan. Among a number of surveys relating to educational questions are two which are worthy of being quoted here in order to show the attitudes of the people towards education. One is the survey conducted by the NHK (Japan Broadcast Corporation) in 1962, and the other that carried out by the Prime Minister's Office in the following year. Both

107

surveys have disclosed some interesting attitudes of the representative adult population of Japan toward education. Some of their findings were as follows.

First, they indicated that the people were concerned with education as much as or even more than with problems of health and living. In the NHK survey a question was asked about which items (a respondent was able to indicate more than one) were most commonly discussed in his or her family. Among the items which were listed, including living, education for children, furniture, hobbies and other cultural activities, housing, retirement, health, business, and social and political questions, education was chosen by 52 per cent of the respondents as occupying the highest place on the list, followed by two other items, health and living, which were both indicated by 49 per cent. The fourth choice was business, and then housing, social and political questions, retirement, hobbies, and furniture in that order. Another question in the same survey asked the respondent to choose one item on the list as his or her own concern, and the answer to this question followed almost the same trend. Education of children was on top, being chosen by 25 per cent of the respondents, followed by health and living, business, housing, etc. Even allowing for the fact that these surveys were on education, and that any educational item in the questions was therefore liable to receive more attention, it is still interesting to see that the people regard the education of children as one of their greatest concerns, equalled only by health and living, and superseding other questions such as business, social and political questions, etc.

Equally keen interest was expressed in education by the respondents themselves, in the answers to another question in the same survey, asking if they were willing at this moment to receive education of any kind. Except for the older generations, in which only 15 per cent of those over 70 and 39 per cent of those between 60 and 69 answered positively, the majority of the rest of the population, in particular those belonging to the younger generations, reacted quite positively. For example, among those of the 20–24 age group 85 per cent answered yes, as did 86 per cent of those of between 30–34 years. Among the different professions, those in clerical and technical work showed the keenest interest for their own education, as 89% of them answered positively. They were followed by professional and managerial groups, of whom 83 per cent gave a positive answer. Even 66 per cent of housewives were interested in receiving education. Among those who had previously received education up to elementary level, 53 per cent responded positively while 75 per cent positive response was given by those who had received academic secondary education and above. Thus, although the pattern varied somewhat according to age, occupation, and educational background, it can safely be said that the Japanese as a whole are keen to continue their education after the age of formal education.

With regard to education for their children, both surveys posed similar questions and received similar responses. To the question, "If you have a son and/or daughter, up to which level of education do you wish to provide for them?", 68 per cent of the respondents of the NHK survey wished their sons to complete university education, and only 2 per cent were content to let their sons complete only compulsory education up to 15 years old. With regard to the daughters, 33 per cent of the parents wished to send their daughters to a university, while 4 per cent thought education only up to the compulsory age was sufficient. In the survey of the Prime Minister's Office, 52 per cent of the respondents wanted to send their sons to universities, while only 1 per cent did not want their sons to receive more than compulsory education. In the same survey, 28 per cent of the respondents wished to send their daughters to universities, while 3 per cent were satisfied with their daughters being educated only up to the compulsory education level.

Thus, according to these surveys, almost all Japanese parents are eager to give their children education beyond compulsory education age except for a small minority who happen to be less-educated residents in rural areas. Furthermore, a considerable portion of the parents (in the case of boys more than half, and a third or more in the case of girls) wanted to send their children to universities or other higher institutions.

In order to analyse such a wish on the part of the parents in relation to their economic capacity, a question was put in the Prime Minister's Office survey in which the respondents were requested to indicate one of the six alternatives to complete the sentence:

"I want to give my children higher education:
  (a) at all cost;
  (b) even if the burden is heavy;
  (c) up to a certain limit;

(d) if it is not too much burden;

(e) if I can afford it;

(f) don't know."

Twenty-four per cent of the parents expressed the intention of giving their boys higher education "at all cost", 21 per cent "even if the burden is heavy" and another 51 per cent "up to a certain limit". In the case of daughters they seemed to be less enthusiastic, although the trend was about the same. Seven per cent of them answered "at all cost", 16 per cent "even if the burden is heavy", and 57 per cent "up to a certain limit". In both cases only 3 per cent responded "if I can afford it".

The answers given to the question why they wished to give their children higher education were interesting. In the Prime Minister's Office survey, 24 per cent of them chose, where boys were concerned, the item "to give them professional knowledge and skills", and 18 per cent for general culture. Twelve per cent of them would send their sons to higher institutions since everyone else would. Others chose more pragmatic motives: "it is useful anyway", "it is disadvantageous to be without it", "to get good jobs", were each chosen by 8 per cent. Only 2 per cent chose "because my children like to study". For daughters, 14 per cent of parents would do so in order to give them general culture, followed by 8 per cent who expected their daughters to gain professional knowledge and skill, and 4 per cent "because everyone else does". The pragmatic reasons were chosen by between 1 and 2 per cent of them. One per cent gave as their reason that their daughters liked to study.

In summing up the results of these surveys it may be observed that with certain variations according to age, areas of residence, educational background, and sex, the parents have a considerable interest in their own and their children's education. With regard to the latter, almost all the adult population wished to give their children (or possible children) education beyond compulsory education, up to university level in a considerable proportion of cases. They were eager to send them, despite a certain financial strain. Indeed, a sizeable proportion of them wished to do so at all costs. They felt that higher education was either good or useful for their children.

The findings of these surveys coincide with those of other similar surveys, and taken together with them, reaffirmed previous assessments of the population's general aspirations in education. It would, of course, be erroneous to attribute this aspiration or "zeal" for education of the Japanese people to their innate characteristics. Nor would it be true to say that such a trait is to be found only in Japanese society. The truth is that this is a socio-psychological phenomenon which can be created under certain social and psychological conditions, and that, given such conditions, any society can find among its members an equally strong zeal for education. Such conditions would be first, that education in a given society provides an important means for social upward mobility, and second, that the opportunity for such education is fairly widely open to any member of the society. It is, however, still true that Japanese society offers a classic example of this phenomenon, if not an exclusive one.

BACKGROUND OF THE HIGH LEVEL OF ASPIRATION TO EDUCATION

In Japanese society, education has long been considered an effective way of climbing up the social ladder. In the feudalistic Tokugawa period between the seventeenth and nineteenth centuries, when the class system rigidly existed, such intellectual professions as scholars and priests enjoyed their high social status despite the fact that some of them had risen from the common social level only by means of education. In the later Tokugawa regime, both the central and local feudal governments adopted the policy of recruiting able youths of the lower rank of the ruling warrior class, and even of the more common population, by opening the government schools to them. This policy encouraged the people to believe that education would give them a good opportunity of social success.

The Meiji government, which in fact was established by these new leaders who rose through education, adopted the same policy as soon as they took over power in the latter part of the nineteenth century. For one thing, they needed a substantial number of government officials who were capable of absorbing the new Western knowledge and techniques and of running the government after the Western model. The first national school plan of 1872 indicated the establishment of the systems of universal primary education and of the selective secondary and higher education. Only five years later the University of Tokyo was set up and was soon renamed the Imperial University, with the deliberate purpose of training the officials of the Imperial Government. Among the faculties, the Faculty of Law was given the highest status as it was to produce the law-makers and executives for the government. The Dean of the Faculty of Law was at the same time the President of the Imperial University, and the graduates of this faculty were exempt from the government examination on entering the service. Other faculties were also meant to provide the specialist administrators for the government, and the faculties of engineering, agriculture, medicine, and economics, also sent their graduates with technical expertise to the government.

Thus, until the early twentieth century, when other imperial universities as well as other forms of higher education were created, the Imperial University of Tokyo enjoyed its monopoly in producing the government's privileged élite group. Even after this monopoly was broken, the superior position of the Imperial University of Tokyo still remained, and its successor, the present University of Tokyo, still enjoys this inheritance. By 1940 the number of universities had increased to 47, and in addition there were 225 non-degree granting colleges in various specialized fields of arts, science, commerce, engineering, agriculture, medicine, pharmacy, etc. They formed a kind of hierarchical pyramid: according to the foundation status, the imperial universities of Tokyo and others on the top, followed by the government and private universities, and then by colleges in order of status. Their hierarchical status was also determined by the kind of field in which the graduates would be employed. Under the bureaucratic system of pre-World-War-II Japan, the imperial universities, because of historical incidents, almost monopolized the supply of higher government officials and thus occupied the highest status. Other government and private universities which were created later and which produced in the main the leaders of private business and industry were considered as second class. As business and industry expanded later, many graduates of imperial and other superior universities entered these private fields to take key posts direct from university or after serving in the government for many years.

How the graduates of universities formed themselves into the élite group of Japanese society was shown chronologically in a study conducted by Professor Aso Yutaka based on several editions of a Japanese *Who's Who*. According to Professor Azabu's study, university graduates formed only 20 per cent of the élite group in 1903. The percentage remained about the same until the latter part of the 1920s; 25 per cent in 1911 and 1915 respectively, and 21 per cent in 1921. In the late 1920s the figure increased rapidly; 39 per cent in 1928, 40 per cent in 1934, and 50 per cent in 1941. After the end of World War II, university graduates became the majority of the élite group; 74 per cent in 1948 and 1953 respectively, 81 per cent in 1957, and 83 per cent in 1964. Over the half century which the study covered, the nature of the élite group in the Japanese society has thus changed; the traditional types in the élite, such as aristocrats and landowners, decreased in number and finally disappeared, while the intellectual élite, such as professors, educators, and artists, increased. The business leaders and bureaucrats constantly occupied an important and substantial part of the élite group. While admitting the change in the nature of the élite, it is still significant to note that the universities played an increasingly important role in producing the national élite of Japan.

This increasing role of higher education in the formation of the national élite had an important effect upon the psychology of the people with regard to their attitude towards education. It is true that these élite formed only a small minority of the nation and were very far from the majority of ordinary people. Nevertheless, the existence of such an élite group, however small in number, who had achieved their positions by means of education, had a symbolic meaning for the populace. For one thing, Japanese society consisted of various strata (layers) of élite groups: under the top élite group in the nation existed many different levels of national and local élite groups. In such lower echelons of the élite group existed the same tendency as could be observed at the top national level. Thus ordinary people could see the effect of higher education in determining the social status, not only at the top national level in a more or less symbolic way, but also more directly through their own neighbouring situation.

Furthermore, the opportunity for attaining such higher education was fairly widely opened to everybody in Japan. The national system of education of 1872, which formed a basis for the further development, consisted of a universal common elementary education and of a secondary and higher education by selection, which should come after the common elementary education. The transition from elementary to secondary and from secondary to higher education was determined by competitive examinations. Unlike the contemporary European systems, there was no privileged self-contained preparatory—secondary—university system in which the children of a particular social group could complete their higher education. It is true that in the later period the wealthy parents of Japan found a way of sending their children up to universities through private schools and universities. It is also true that a sociological law existed in Japanese society by which the children of the privileged families had more opportunity for higher education than those of less-privileged ones, even taking into account the public system of education.

Nevertheless, the chances of higher education beyond elementary schooling existed even for those less privileged, and if they were intelligent enough to pass the selective examinations and lucky enough to find some financial support by means of scholarship or work, they could complete their university education through the public system of education, in which the cost of education was at a minimum. It was therefore not too rare for people to find a boy in a village or in the same neighbourhood who completed his higher education and entered the promised land of social success. Thus the opportunity for higher education and higher social status existed potentially for everyone in Japanese society, although he himself might not enjoy it.

Such an attitude toward a successful career and higher education has been greatly reinforced in post-World-War-II Japanese society. The egalitarianism of the new democratic Constitution has encouraged the people to regard themselves as being equally qualified to lead this successful life. The democratization of various social institutions has certainly broadened the chances of joining the élite groups for ordinary people who previously had to consider such an opportunity as being a mere possibility. In this respect, the democratized schools and universities have played an important role.

Under the democratic principle of equal opportunity for all, the post-war school system of 1947 has extended the school-leaving age from 12 to 15, and given to all boys and girls belonging to these age groups education in common "middle schools". The upper secondary schools have been named "high schools" in the new system, and provide both academic and vocational courses. Unlike the pre-war secondary education system, which allowed only the graduates of academic secondary and post secondary schools, which were called "middle schools" and "high schools" respectively, to move up to universities, the graduates of the new high schools, regardless of their courses, are able to proceed to universities. Furthermore, the new system has abolished any statutory distinction between universities and non-degree granting higher institutions, and established a single pattern of "universities".*

The new school system has thus streamlined the educational structure into a single successive one of elementary-middle-high schools and universities, and made universities more easily accessible to the people. The adoption by the new schools of the old renowned titles of academic institutions, particularly that of "middle school" by the common lower secondary school, has had a great psychological effect upon the people. The old psychological barrier of the ordinary population to academic secondary education has been broken by seeing their children in attendance at "middle schools", and once this has been done they have little difficulty in sending their children further to high schools and to universities. It is true that the middle and high schools in the new system have different characters from their pre-war academic counterparts, but this difference matters little in the eyes of most of the people who themselves have no direct experience of either system. The same applies to universities, which having become mass-education institutions, have changed their characters considerably. In fact, one of the sources of the problems in present-day universities lies in this gap between the changing characters of the universities and the somewhat fixed expectations of the people towards the universities. The people still regard the universities as being the most effective channel to lead their children to a higher social status, which is now not too far from their reach. We shall come back to this question later.

There are some other factors which have also stimulated the people's zeal for education in the post-war Japanese society. The economic and industrial expansion since the middle of the 1950s has greatly changed the occupational structure of the society and has increased the demand for qualified personnel in many fields. During the twenty-year period between 1950 and 1970, the percentage in the total labour force engaged in agriculture, forestry, and fishery decreased from 48 per cent to 17 per cent, while those in manufacturing, mining, and construction, and those in

*In 1950 a system of junior colleges was set up as part of the "university" system. The literal translation of Japanese junior college is "short-term university" with the implication that these colleges will provide shorter courses than those of ordinary universities. Later in 1961, a system of technical colleges was created and called "higher specialized schools", and one of the then criticisms was that it set up an inferior higher institution which was not part of the "university" system.

commerce, service industries and public service increased from 22 to 35 per cent and from 30 to 47 per cent in the same period. Such changes involved the processes of reorientation in education and provided a strong incentive to the people for their own education as well as for that of their children.

The changing pattern of family life is another factor. The average number in a family has decreased from 4·9 to 3·7 between 1950 and 1970, and at the same time the percentage of family nuclei in the total population has slightly increased from 60 per cent in 1955 to 62 per cent in 1965. More families live in the cities because of the urbanization process, which increased the percentage of those inhabitants in urban areas with a population of 30,000 and more in the total population from 39 to 69 per cent during the period between 1950 and 1965. These changes, together with general improvements in the living conditions, have provided each family with more time, opportunity, and resources for the education of their children. The effect of these changes has been greater upon women, whose time and energy have been saved to a very large extent and who now have the time to nourish and educate their children. As a result of the co-educational policy and the general improvement of the status of women, the education level of mothers themselves has been improved and, as usual, the higher they have been educated the more they aspire towards higher education for their children.

The development of the mass media is another factor. In 1970 some 117 daily newspapers issued 53 million copies each day, the number equivalent to half of the population of Japan. In the same year 93 per cent of the total households owned television sets. In addition to books published irregularly, in 1969 the number of which amounted to some 26,000 of all kinds, there were some 2500 periodicals, a large proportion of which dealt with education in some way or another. These media constantly bring news and information on education to each family, and while they contribute to raising the public interest in education, they tend to accelerate the people's zeal as it is said "today parents are constantly reminded to be parents".

ADMISSION TO HIGHER EDUCATION – PROBLEMS RELATING TO "ZEAL FOR EDUCATION"

It is possible to say that behind the rapid increase of school population, particularly in upper secondary schools and universities which in the twenty years between 1950 and 1970 increased by 220 and 450 per cent respectively, there has been a "zeal for education" of the people, who have been led to believe by various social and psychological reasons that it is worth striving after education. This "zeal" has certainly had an effect on the educational policies of the government as well as on the educational effort of industry and business circles. As mentioned earlier, the educational expansion which the government has attempted with the support of industry and the business world would not have been achieved if popular interest and enthusiasm were lacking. On the other hand, some educational problems, for which the government is often blamed because of its inadequate handling of them, may also be attributed to this attitude of the people.

No one would disagree that one of the big issues in Japanese education is that of the procedures for admission to high schools and universities. The problem is a long-standing one, and the government — both at central and local levels — has taken various measures including some still in effect, all of which, however, have not yet fully satisfied the people concerned. The problem is a complex one in which the "zeal for education" plays an important role if not the exclusive one.

In the public school system of Japan one has to go through at least four steps of admission procedure before completion of university education; that is to say, a step on entering elementary school, one on moving from there to middle school, one on moving further to high school, and one on entering a university. Of these four steps, the first two, except for special cases which shall be mentioned later, present little difficulty since entrance to compulsory elementary and middle schools is automatic. Only the last two steps involve an element of selection, which is the source of the trouble.

Under the present system, the selection procedure for high school is decided by each prefectural board of education, and thus there are certain local variations. In general, however, it consists of the screening of school records and scholastic achievement tests. The number of school subjects in achievement tests range from three to six, but the majority of prefectures (35 out of 47) give the tests in five subjects. Usually applicants from middle schools are allocated their places in high schools according to their wishes and their rank in the screening list. The range of choice of high schools varies, depending on whether the prefecture in which the student lives adopts a large high school district system in which the high school district covers the whole prefecture and includes all public high schools in this single district, or adopts a middle-size high school district in which the prefecture is divided into a few high school districts, each of which includes more than two high schools. Thus in the former case the range of choice is greater than in the latter. The prefecture of Kyoto adopts a small district system in which the prefecture is divided into a number of high school districts, each of which has only one high school. In this case there is no choice for middle school graduates in the district. The Tokyo prefecture adopts a large district system, but the applicant does not apply to a single high school, but to a local grouping of high schools, and the allocation of the candidate to a particular school in the group is made on a random basis.

For access to university, the Ministry of Education issues a circular as a guideline, but apart from this the exact procedure for admission should be decided by each university. The scholastic achievement tests and school records are the main materials for screening. In general, emphasis is given to the results of achievement tests despite the Ministry's desire to give more weight to school records. The number of school subjects in achievement tests varies, but lies mostly between two and five. The Ministry's recent attempt to introduce standardized achievement and aptitude tests has failed, as it aroused little enthusiasm or co-operation from universities, although its other measure, to encourage universities to admit students, or at least some of them, based on the recommendations of the high schools, has met with some success. The dates for the achievement tests are fixed by the Ministry in such a way that seventy-five state universities are divided into two groups, each of which conducts the tests on the same day, while the other some 300 odd non-state universities are left free to choose the dates at their own convenience. Thus it is possible at least theoretically for an individual applicant to apply to two state universities and as many non-state institutions as he may wish in a single year. It is also possible for him to reapply to the same institutions in as many following years as he wishes.

In the spring (the Japanese school calendar begins in April and ends in March) of 1969 some 1,737,000 students graduated from middle schools. Among them some 1,403,000 applied for high schools and 1,368,000 were admitted. Thus most of the applicants, 98 in a 100, found places in high schools although some found places only in schools of their second choice.

The question of admission to university was much harder. In the same year the number of high school graduates was 1,497,000 out of which 373,000 applied for university and 130,000 for junior college. While 90 per cent of junior college applicants, 117,000 in number, were admitted, only 60 per cent of university applicants, 223,000 in number, were successful. Thus a considerable number of those who did not succeed either abandoned their wish to enter university or, as in the majority of cases, waited for another chance in the following year(s). In fact, in addition to those fresh graduates, there were some 186,000 applicants in the spring of 1969 who had already graduated from high schools (76 per cent of whom had graduated in 1968 and 24 per cent in 1967 or before), and these constituted one-third of the total applicants. As 60 per cent of them were admitted, they also constituted one-third of the total entrants. These reapplicants symbolize the problem.

The rejection of 40 per cent of the applicants may still be justified if one takes the position of selective higher education, which is in accord with the generally accepted policy of the government. It would seem to assure the quality of higher education, although on further analysis this is questionable, as will be discussed later. The problem is in these large number of reapplicants, who are jokingly called "roonin", which means unemployed *samurai* or warriors, implying that these reapplicants are without affiliated universities and are looking eagerly for employment or admission. As the above figures of 1969 indicate, the majority of the failures reapply in the following year to the same university or others, and of these, some unfortunate ones have to apply in further year(s) as they failed again in the second year.

Although their determination and patience might be worthy of praise (indeed, a few years ago a man who entered the University of Tokyo after half a dozen attempts, became a big news item!), it is a great waste, both socially and individually that a large number of youths should spend one year or more just preparing for admission tests after completing full secondary education. This is a symptom of "over zeal for education". These reapplicants have chosen their particular university, usually a good one, which, they believe, can promise them a bright future. Of course, many failures change their objectives in the second year and search for safe admission, but even so a considerable number of them reapply to the same university. In their mind, the admission to, or rather graduation from, these universities will easily compensate them in the long run for the loss of a few years.

On the other hand, there are a large number of applicants who apply to three, four, or more universities in the same year. Again, quoting the figure from 1969, an applicant applied on average 3·5 times. This is another symptom of "zeal for education" as they strive for admission to any university which seems to them to be within easy reach, and which nevertheless will assure them some kind of secure life in the future. Thus it often happens that the competition in the less selective (in the sense of quality) universities is much higher than that in the more selective ones, and therefore the former is more selective (in the sense of quantity) than is the "better" university. This means that the competition is equally stiff for intelligent students and less-intelligent ones. There is also no difference between them in the waste of energy, time, and money.

It is not only waste, but also harm from a genuinely educational point of view. As mentioned earlier, the admission to universities usually depends on the results of a few days tests in a few selected subjects, and these tests are usually given to eliminate, rather than to select, the candidates easily. Thus it is generally believed that to pass the tests certain skills or techniques are required in addition to the mastery of subject matter. Thus a lot of time is spent on the mastering of special skills, including the knowledge of trends in tests, some difficult points, etc. This is certainly an additional burden to students as well as to teachers, and for the proper learning—teaching process this is useless and even harmful. As preparation is made only for those subjects to be tested, other subjects tend to be neglected. It is more so in other school activities, which are not related to the admission tests, but which are, however, equally important for a balanced development in the personality of the young person.

This also involves a question of social equality. Preparation for the admission tests costs time and money. In regular schooling in high schools, students may be required to buy additional books and materials, and not a small number of them take additional courses after school hours or in the summer provided by high schools, private schools, or preparatory schools, which are set up specifically to prepare students for the admission tests. Most reapplicants register with day courses of such preparatory schools. Not all parents can easily afford such expenses, although many would sacrifice themselves for their children as indicated by the opinion survey quoted earlier. Because of such financial reasons, many able youths may have given up proceeding to higher education. This is more likely in the case of girls, in whose higher education the parents are less likely to invest. This often causes disciplinary problems among high school students, particularly between the privileged ones in high education and those underprivileged.

One of the most serious problems is that such waste, harm, and unfairness permeate down into middle schools and even elementary schools, and produce many undesirable byproducts. In the middle schools, the competition for access to high school education is less than that for universities. Nonetheless, the problem is equally serious, particularly in considering the ages of the pupils involved. The same kind of waste, harm, and unfairness in the preparation for admission exists in this stage. As is the case for high school students, more able pupils in middle schools choose the renowned high schools whose prestige has been gained by the high success rate in university admission in the previous years. According to a survey, there are some 160 renowned high schools, the majority of which are public schools with a sense of tradition, but which also include some half-dozen schools attached to state universities and a dozen private schools. They constitute only a very small minority of some 4000 high schools, but their graduates are said to compose two-thirds of the most renowned seven state universities.

Many state and private high schools have middle school sections attached to them, and it is commonly agreed that their high success rates are due to their six years' continuous education. As they take pupils at the beginning of both the high and middle school stages, the preparation to enter these and other renowned, and other less-famous high schools, begins right at the elementary school stage. Although the number of elementary pupils preparing for admission tests for such state and private middle schools is small (some 4 per cent in 1969), the effect of their existence upon elementary education is not negligible. Parental pressure has already been observed to orient elementary education into more preparation for admission to the higher stages of education.

Unfortunately, there are already renowned elementary schools which have gained their fame by their "effective education" in sending their graduates to famous secondary schools and universities. Again, the same waste, harm, and unfairness exist in elementary education although in different forms and degrees. Such phenomena as cramming, heavy workload, frequent tests, and heavy homework are reported in some schools. Those parents who are not satisfied with their children's school work provide additional tutorial work for them after school hours at home or at private schools which are set up specifically for this purpose. Such pathological cases as "schoolphobia" in which children refuse to go to school, commit suicide, display violence, and other maladjusted symptoms, are often attributed to this preparation-orientated pressure upon children.

There should be no misunderstanding of the fact that many teachers, parents, and administrators have been striving for a remedy to the problem, aware of its graveness. Much effort has been made by them to improve the systems of admission, guidance, and instruction in schools. Such organizations as the departmental Committee on University Admission of the Ministry of Education and the Association of State Universities have repeatedly made recommendations on the improvement of the admission system. Test material has been improved to make it a more reliable basis for screening. Guidance has been regarded as an important activity in high and middle schools. Attempts have been made to improve the curriculum and teaching methods in order to develop the abilities and skills of children in the proper way, which at the same time should enable them to pass the tests. Nevertheless, no satisfactory solution has yet been achieved. For one thing, the problem is deeply related to the success-oriented structure of Japanese society. As long as the people believe that the success of their career is based on education, they will hold on to their "zeal for education", and thus the problems relating to admission and preparation may continue in some way or another.

The real problem thus lies in the relationship between school and society, or more specifically between universities and the government and businesses, which recruit the graduates of universities. Although the civil service examinations are open to any university graduates, a number of major firms close their doors except to graduates of certain renowned universities. In such firms there often exist what are called "academic cliques" which have strong influence upon the personnel policies of the firms. An individual employee may be treated favourably or unfavourably depending on which clique he belongs to. Nor do government offices escape from the blame of "academic cliques". Many inside stories tell how certain posts have been filled by a group of one clique or another. These stories, true or untrue, reaffirm the popular belief in there being superior chances for the graduates of renowned universities.

It is true that, thanks to the democratization of society, such "academic cliques" have diminished in importance. The merit system has been adopted more and more in offices and firms. This is partly due to the rapid development of knowledge and techniques which require constant re-education or life-long education, and diminish the significance of the initial university education. The swift progress in the business and industrial world has caused a scarcity of qualified personnel, and thus offices and firms have become obliged to broaden their basis for recruitment in search of such qualified personnel. This has given an opportunity to those who, despite their abilities, were previously handicapped because of a less-favourable academic background. Therefore, Morita Akio, the president of Sony Corporation, had reason to pronounce the uselessness of an academic career in this changing industrial period and to support constant re-education and promotion by merit. These trends should certainly affect the people's attitude towards education. At the moment, however, little change has been observed, as it is said that traditional belief dies hard. On the contrary, the popular feeling of insecurity which has been caused by rapid social change tends to encourage them to cling to their old belief in "zeal for education" even harder.

It is, of course, erroneous to attribute all evils in contemporary education to this "zeal" or "over-zeal" of the people, as it is only one of the factors working in educational problems. Nevertheless, and in particular if one considers the positive contribution of the people's enthusiasm to the development of Japanese education, such "zeal for education" is an important factor which cannot be overlooked in understanding Japanese education.

CHAPTER 7

The National System of Education

The democratic principle which guides present-day Japanese education stipulates that all people shall be given equal opportunities to receive education according to their abilities. Therefore the prime purpose of the national system of education is to ensure the people such opportunities with as much certainty as possible. In the preceding chapters it was observed to what extent historical, political, economic, and social factors have affected the moulding of the present Japanese system of national education. In this chapter we will make a survey of this system and will attempt to examine the educational opportunities it should provide for the people.

According to the Japanese idea, the national system of education includes all educational activities of a public nature. Broadly speaking, it consists of the formal school system and the less formal system of social education or what is usually called out-of-school education. The two parliamentary acts, the School Education Law of 1947 and the Social Education Law of 1949 and the related ministerial regulations respectively define the areas, functions, personnel, and institutions for both school and social education. This provides standardization for the national system, which ensures a common level of education throughout the country, while leaving relatively little room for local variations. There is only one national system of education and the local differences exist only within this standardized framework.

From the administrative point of view, the schools and other educational institutions are divided into three categories — state, local public, and private. The difference between them, however, is purely connected with administration and finance. With regard to the structure of the institutions, the content of the education and the qualifications of the

124

teaching personnel, they are all subject to the laws and regulations. The only exception is in the field of religious education, which is the privilege of private institutions. Thus the use of the word "private" may be misleading if the word suggests that the private schools and other educational institutions are outside the public or national system of education. On the contrary, the Japanese private institutions constitute an important part of the nation's educational system.

Since the 1947 reform the Japanese school system has become fairly simple compared with the previous multiple track system.* Fundamentally it is the so-called 6–3–3–4 system, i.e. six years' elementary school (following one to three years' kindergarten), three years' middle school, three years' high school, and four years' university (with two to five years' graduate school). At the time of the 1947 reform, this single-ladder system was considered to be best suited to achieve the goal of equal opportunities for all which was set by the Fundamental Law of Education. In order to meet the demands from different sections of society, however, the system was later slightly modified, and a certain degree of diversification in late secondary and higher education developed within it.

The Social Education Law defines social education as the general term for organized programmes of educational activities for young people and adults, including programmes of physical education and recreation, and excluding those provided in the curriculum of schools, colleges, and universities. The facilities for social education include citizen's public halls, libraries, museums, youth centres, cultural and nature centres for children, and public facilities for physical and recreational activities.

School and university facilities and various forms of mass media are also used in social education. Educational activities are organized in adult classes, home education classes, classes for women and young people, university extension courses, and correspondence courses. As a kind of social education, industrial training is provided for young people and adults at training centres within factories and at public centres.

In Japan, as in other industrialized nations, national education is a large enterprise with regard to the number of people involved, the institutions concerned, and the money spent. In 1970 some 23 million children and young people attended 60,000 schools, colleges, and universities. In

*Refer to Charts I and II in the Appendix.

addition, some 5 million young people and adults attended 92,000 courses for adult education. Those engaged in teaching in such institutions amount to 1½ million, and those in administration and management numbered over 40,000. Thus, to sum up, nearly 30 per cent of the nation was directly concerned with education. If one counted the large number of parents naturally very concerned about the education of their children, this percentage would be further increased. There were also a large number of individuals engaged on educational activities outside the official educational circles, such as in industry, the mass media, the armed forces, etc. The amount of money which the Japanese people spent on education in 1968 was estimated at approximately 3 billion yen, or 5·9 per cent of the gross national product of Japan in the same year.

Some twenty-five years ago, in 1950, approximately 19 million children and young people attended schools, colleges, and universities, and over 1½ million attended classes for social education. A comparison of 1950 and 1970 figures shows the areas in which the expansion was greatest during this period. As Table 2 indicates, as the number of pupils in elementary and middle schools decreased owing to the general decrease of the birth rate, a notable increase occurred in other areas such as kindergartens, high schools, universities and junior colleges, miscellaneous schools, and schools for special education. It is generally agreed that such a trend will continue further.

Table 2

	Number of Students (in thousands)	
	1950	1970
Kindergartens	225	1,675
Elementary schools	11,191	9,494
Middle schools	3,333	4,717
High schools	1,935	4,232
Junior colleges	15	263
Universities	225	1,407
Special schools	17	52
Miscellaneous schools	487	1,353

ELEMENTARY AND SECONDARY EDUCATION

Pre-school education

The major institution for children at the pre-school age is kindergarten. Its purpose is prescribed by the School Education Law as that of bringing up young children and developing their minds and bodies while providing a suitable environment. Kindergartens admit children aged 3, 4, or 5, offering them respectively three-, two- or one-year courses. The Curriculum Standards for Kindergartens issued by the Ministry of Education in 1956 and 1964 stipulate that the contents of kindergarten education should cover six areas, i.e. health, social life, nature, language, music, and art, in order to achieve the following objectives of kindergarten education prescribed by the School Education Law:

(1) To cultivate everyday habits necessary for a sound, safe, and happy life, and to effect a harmonious development of bodily functions.

(2) To make children experience a group life in the kindergarten and to cultivate willingness to take part in it as well as to encourage the spirit of co-operation and independence.

(3) To cultivate a right understanding of and a right attitude towards the surrounding social life and happenings.

(4) To guide the child in the proper use of language and to foster an interest in fairy tales and picture books.

(5) To cultivate an interest in creative expression through music, dance, pictures, and other means.

As observed earlier, the development of kindergartens in the 1950s and 1960s was remarkable; the number of pupils enrolled increased more than seven times during this twenty-year period. In the same period the number of kindergartens increased more than five times. The percentage of children in the first grade in elementary schools who had received kindergarten education also increased from 8·9 per cent in 1950 to 53·7 per cent in 1970.

Despite these increases, however, the opportunities of Japanese children for a kindergarten education were still limited in comparison with those of more advanced countries such as France, the United States, and England (which, of course, takes all children aged 5 into compulsory infant schools). This backwardness was due mainly to the previous lack of government interest in this area. It was only in 1964, when the Ministry of

Education set up, for the first time, a seven-year plan for the promotion of kindergarten education, that some effect was seen in a raised attendance rate as mentioned above. As in 1970, less than 40 per cent of the kindergartens were maintained by public authorities, thus leaving a larger part of kindergarten education to private voluntary efforts.

This gap has been filled partially by other public institutions for young children, namely day nurseries. While kindergartens are under the jurisdiction of public education authorities, day nurseries are under the supervision of the public welfare authorities. The Child Welfare Law of 1947 stipulated the establishment of day nurseries which were to take care of children aged 0–5 years inclusive, who were in need of institutional care. Most of the day nurseries are run by local authorities. In 1970 the number of children in some 14,000 day nurseries was 1,180,000 – this number constituting some 22 per cent of those in the age group 0–5 years.

As the children in kindergartens and day nurseries increased in number, some sort of co-ordination between the two institutions became necessary. Thus in 1963 a circular was issued jointly by the Ministries of Education and of Welfare which suggested that the children aged 4 and 5 in the day nurseries should receive similar educational care as those in kindergartens.

Elementary schools

All children who have passed their sixth birthday are required to receive elementary education at six-year elementary schools. The aims of elementary education have already been quoted in Chapter 3. In short, the elementary school aims at giving children between the ages of 6 and 12 education and training for basic attitudes, knowledge, skill, and ability in accordance with the stages of their mental and physical development.

The elementary school curriculum prescribed in the Course of Study covers eight regular subjects, moral education, and special activities. The eight subjects are the Japanese language, social studies, arithmetic, science, music, art and craft, home-making, and physical education. The special activities include (a) pupil activities, such as school and class assemblies and club activities, (b) school events, such as ceremonies, literary exercises and exhibitions, athletic meetings, and school excursions, and (c) other activities such as guidance on etiquette at school lunch, utilization of school libraries, health education, and safety education. Lessons on regular subjects and moral education must be given for thirty-five weeks or more per year. The hours allocated to each subject in a weekly schedule are shown in Table 3.

Table 3

Subjects	Grade					
	I	II	III	IV	V	VI
Japanese language	7	9	8	8	7	7
Social studies	2	2	3	4	4	4
Arithmetic	3	4	5	6	6	6
Science	2	2	3	3	4	4
Music	3	2	2	2	2	2
Art and craft	3	2	2	2	2	2
Home-making	—	—	—	—	2	2
Physical education	3	3	3	3	3	3
Moral education	1	1	1	1	1	1
Total	24	25	27	29	31	31

Since the first provisional Course of Study for Elementary Schools was issued in 1947 it has been revised a few times. The 1958 version, which had effect from 1961 to 1971, laid special emphasis upon the following points:

(a) the strengthening of moral education;

(b) the upgrading of basic scholastic abilities;

(c) the advancement of education for science and technology;

(d) the improvement of teaching of geography and history.

The latest revised Course of Study of 1968, which came into effect in 1971, had the intention of improving the elementary school curriculum in the following points;

(a) to make the curriculum more harmonized and integrated so as to ensure a child the development of a well-balanced personality;

(b) to give more emphasis to basic and essential subject-matter so as to alleviate excessive work-load for pupils and to keep the content of teaching abreast with the progress of society;

(c) to give individual schools more flexibility in determining the allocation of hours for each subject;

(d) to adapt the content of teaching more to the differing abilities and aptitudes of individual pupils;

(e) to integrate the curricula of elementary and secondary schools.

The teaching at elementary schools has been much improved. Although the traditional methods of teaching with textbooks, chalk, and blackboard are still commonly seen, many new methods and teaching aids are introduced to stimulate the pupils' initiative in the learning process. In 1969 the average number of pupils per class was 33, a number which was considered still too large to permit the teacher to pay attention to individual pupils. Unlike the secondary school, in the elementary school a classroom teacher generally covers all subjects. However, there is an attempt to introduce specialized teaching at the higher grades of elementary schools.

Since 1920 the enrolment rate of children between the ages of 6 and 12 in elementary schools has been over 99 per cent. In 1970 it was 99·83 per cent. The remaining 0·17 per cent was mostly those who were exempt from enrolling in school because of heavy mental or physical handicap. There is also the problem of lengthy absenteeism — those absent for more than fifty days out of a 240-day school year. These problems will be discussed later.

Middle schools

Japanese secondary education is divided into two stages. The first stage is provided in the three-year middle school which all children, upon completion of their elementary education are required to attend until the end of the third year of their course, during which time they should have reached the age of 15. The aim of the middle school is prescribed by the School Education Law as that of giving pupils general education according to the development of their minds and bodies on the basis of the education given in the elementary school. The three main objectives of middle school education are the following:

(a) to cultivate the qualities necessary to be a member of a society and the State;

(b) to cultivate fundamental knowledge and skill in the vocations required in society, the attitude of respect for labour, and the ability to select a future course according to individual capacity;

(c) to promote social activities in and out of school, to cultivate right feeling, and to foster fair judgement.

In developing the curricula in individual schools, some specialization is introduced into the school programme in order to cope with different aptitudes and interests of the pupils. The subjects taught include such compulsory ones as the Japanese language, social studies, mathematics, science, music, fine arts, health and physical education, industrial arts (for boys) or home-making (for girls), and moral education. The elective subjects include foreign languages (mostly English), and vocational subjects such as agriculture, industry, commerce, fisheries, and home-making. The choice of the elective subjects is determined, not by individual children, but by local education authorities in the light of local needs and the pupils' abilities and prospects. The standard number of weekly school hours for middle schools is given in Table 4.

Table 4

	Grade		
	VII	VIII	IX
Required subjects			
Japanese language	5	5	5
Social studies	4	4	5
Mathematics	4	4	4
Science	4	4	4
Music	2	2	1
Fine arts	2	2	1
Health and physical education	3+	3+	3+
Industrial arts (Home-making)	3	3	3
Moral education	1	1	1
Special activities	1	1	1
Elective subjects	4	4	4
(e.g. Foreign languages	3	3	3)
(A vocational subject	1	1	2)
Total	34	34	33

The above time allocation is prescribed in the Course of Study for Middle Schools of 1969, which has been in effect since 1971. For the past twenty years it has been revised a few times on the same principles as that applied to the curriculum revision for elementary schools. For middle schools, however, special consideration has been given to the changing nature of middle school pupils. In 1951, when the Course of Study for Middle Schools was first revised, only 46 per cent of middle graduates moved to high schools. In 1962, when the second revision took effect, the corresponding figure increased to 64 per cent. In 1970 it reached 85 per cent, and an annual increase at the rate of some 2 per cent was expected. With such a change in prospect, the immediate vocational preparation became less important, while the articulation with the high school curricula acquired weight in the middle school programme.

High schools

The second stage of secondary education is mainly provided in the high school, attendance at which is, however, not compulsory. The admission of middle school graduates to the high school involved serious problems, which have been already mentioned in the previous chapter.

The aim of the high school is stipulated by the School Education Law as that of giving pupils general and specialized education appropriate to their mental and physical development. Since some of its graduates are expected to continue their education in the higher institutions, while others leave to start work, the high school has to provide both preparatory and terminal education. In order to meet with these different needs, the Course of Study for High Schools of 1960, which was in effect between 1963 and 1973, suggested various courses. Fundamentally the high school curricula are classified into general and specialized courses. The general courses are further divided into the terminal general course, the academic preparatory course, and a course combining these. The specialized courses include the courses for music and fine arts, and the vocational courses such as agriculture, engineering, business studies, fisheries, and home-making. These vocational courses are further specialized into various branches of these vocations.

The minimum requirements for all students, regardless of course, are that they cover two subjects in Japanese language, four subjects in social studies and basic mathematics, two subjects in science, health, physical education, one foreign language, and one subject in fine arts. Those in the general courses have to take additional subjects among the areas mentioned above and, for girls in particular, also home-making. Those in the specialized courses take the additional subjects in their specialities. The actual requirements vary: Table 5 is only one example of the academic preparatory course.

Table 5

	Grade and number of credits[1]			
	X	XI	XII	Total
Modern Japanese	3	2	2	7
Advanced Japanese classics I	2	3		5
Advanced Japanese classics II			3	3
Ethics-civics		2		2
Political science—economics			2	2
Japanese history			3	3
Advanced world history		2	2	4
Advanced geography	4			4
Basic mathematics	5			5
Advanced mathematics I		5		5
Advanced mathematics II			5	5
Advanced physics		3	2	5
Advanced chemistry		2	2	4
Biology	4			4
Earth science	2			2
Health	4,2[2]	3	3	9,7[2]
Physical education		1	1	2
Fine arts	2			2
Advanced fine arts		2	2	4
Advanced English	5	5	5	15
Home-making	2[2]	2[2]	2[2]	6[2]
Special activities	1	1	1	3
Total	32	31 / 33[2]	30	93 / 95[2]

[1] One credit consists of thirty-five school hours.
[2] For girls only.

In 1970 some one-third of the high schools were "comprehensive", offering both general and specialized courses, while more than one-third of them offered only general courses and the others only specialized courses. During the 1960s the trend was towards an increase in the specialized high schools in response to industrial needs.

Opportunities for high school education are also provided through the part-time and correspondence courses. The requirements for graduation in these courses are the same as those of the full-time courses, but the duration of the courses is four years or more. In 1970 one-quarter of the high schools offered both full-time and part-time courses, while 13 per cent of them, 611 in number, offered only part-time courses. The correspondence courses were provided in 585 high schools, out of which 14 were specialized in correspondence education. The percentage of part-time and correspondence course students of the total high school student population in 1970 was 8·4 and 3·6 per cent respectively. In 1960 the corresponding figures were 15·7 and 1·9 per cent, indicating the general decrease in the proportion of part-time students in particular.

In Japan there is no secondary school-leaving examination as such. Upon completion of the graduation requirements, the student receives a diploma. The rate of failures or drop-outs around the middle of the 1960s was 5–6 per cent for boys in full-time courses, 30–37 per cent for boys in part-time courses, and some 20 per cent for girls in part-time courses. As has already been observed in the previous chapter, the high school graduates must pass the competitive entrance examination set by the individual universities or colleges in order to have an opportunity to receive higher education.

EDUCATIONAL OPPORTUNITIES FOR THE UNDERPRIVILEGED

Here the term underprivileged is used in a broad sense, including not only those who are physically and mentally handicapped but also those who are disadvantaged because of social reasons.

Special Education for the Physically and Mentally Handicapped

The educational institution for these children is the special school, the aim of which is defined by the School Education Law of 1947 as being that of providing physically or mentally handicapped children with an education on the same level as the kindergarten, the elementary school, the junior high school, or the senior high school, and at the same time giving them necessary skills and knowledge to supplement their deficiencies. Three kinds of special school are the school for the blind, the school for the deaf, and the nursing school for those handicapped in some other way. Each special school consists of an elementary department and a middle department. It may have a kindergarten and/or a high department. The curriculum for each department includes the same kinds of school subjects offered in other schools of the same level, and the subjects and activities are designed for the particular needs of the handicapped children.

Special classes are also provided within the regular elementary school and the middle school for mentally defectives, the crippled, the physically weak, the partially blind, and those with difficulties in hearing. The number of special schools and classes and their enrolment in 1969 are shown in Table 6.

Table 6

	Number of institutions	Enrolment
Schools for the blind	75	9,722
Schools for the deaf	107	17,288
Nursing schools	224	23,173
Special classes	14,527	122,916
		173,099

According to the estimate made by the Ministry of Education in the same year, there were some 529,000 children of school age in need of special education. Those in special schools or classes were only one-third of the handicapped, and the rest were in regular schools without, in most cases, the proper educational care necessary for them. The enrolment rate in special schools differs according to the kind of deficiency. The rate for the deaf and those with a hearing deficiency was some 75 per cent, the highest percentage, while that for speech impediment was only 4 per cent, the lowest. Those for the crippled, the partially or totally blind, the mentally retarded, and the physically weak were 54, 44, 41 and 8 per cent respectively.

The small enrolment rate in special schools and classes is primarily due to lack of facilities. Under the present policy of the Ministry of Education, the attendance at special schools is compulsory only for the blind and the deaf, and thus only the establishment of schools for the blind and the deaf is mandatory for the local education authorities. Although the Ministry provides them with subsidies for building nursing schools, the facilities for the handicapped children other than the blind and the deaf are still less than sufficient.

Another reason for the small enrolment is the financial burden of the parents. For them the State and local authorities provide financial assistance in such items as textbooks and articles of stationery, school meals, boarding, transportation, and school excursions. The assistance is given according to the parents' income. In the middle of the 1960s a half of the pupils in attendance at special schools received full assistance, and some 40 per cent received partial assistance.

Partly related to the financial question, there is some reluctance among a certain group of parents to send their children to special schools. Although diminishing, there is still some prejudice among society against the handicapped, in particular the mentally retarded. As a move of sympathy with the parents, it is proposed to mix the handicapped children with others in the regular classes. The supporting idea is that, with proper handling, the mixed class provides the best opportunities for the children and parents concerned to break through the social prejudice against the handicapped.

The ministerial estimate quoted earlier of handicapped children of school age excludes some 20,000 children who are exempt from schooling because of severe deficiencies. The exemption is judged by the local education authorities under the standards set by the Ministry of Education. There is some argument as to whether these standards are not too inflexible or severe so that some handicapped children are excluded unfairly from receiving an education.

At present such severe cases are mostly cared for in the welfare service establishments run by both public and private bodies according to the Child Welfare Law and related regulation laid down by the Ministry of Welfare. For the physically handicapped children of school age there were 229 establishments with a total of 20,000 children boarding in 1970. In the same year, for the mentally defectives, there were 308 boarding and 88 day establishments with 22,135 and 3605 children respectively. These establishments offer a triple care, i.e. medical, social, and educational to the handicapped. Some of them, which are recognized by the education authorities as special schools, provide educational facilities including qualified teachers. For those who are not in the establishments, the 139 child-guidance centres offer home visiting services.

Assistance to the Underprivileged

Although the Constitution of Japan guarantees equal opportunities of education for all, certain groups of children are *de facto* underprivileged for different social reasons, one of which is poverty. Despite the general prosperity of Japanese society, some children of the lower income families suffer from poverty and are deprived of their chance to receive education. According to the estimate made by the Ministry of Education, some

64,000 children of school age were absent from school for more than fifty days during the school year of 1969. The majority of these were due to illness, but a significant proportion of 2300 were absent from school for economic reasons. Under the Daily Life Protection Law, a total of 1,340,000 persons received some kind of public assistance in 1970, and out of this number 260,000 children were offered educational assistance to cover expenses for school supplies, transportation to school, clothes and other goods necessary to attend school, school meals, school excursions, medical treatment, and school security insurance.

For the high school and college students, public assistance is given in the form of scholarships. A national scholarship programme is provided by the Japan Scholarship Society, a public corporation with a state subsidy. In 1970 the percentage of high school students who received scholarships from the Society was 2·3 and that of undergraduate students was 120. In the same year 49·2 per cent of masters course students and 74·1 per cent of doctoral students received the Society's scholarships. Parallel with this state programme, some other public and private organizations offer financial assistance to the needy student. In 1967 some 410,000 students were given scholarships from various sources, and the majority (76 per cent) were assisted by the state, while 12 per cent and 10 per cent were assisted by local authorities and private foundations and individuals respectively.

The rapid programme of urbanization in recent years has emphasized the problems of other groups of underprivileged children, namely those living in the densely populated cities, on the one hand, and those in the sparsely populated rural areas, on the other. In such metropolitan areas as Tokyo and Osaka and several other large industrial cities, children suffer from various environmental defects such as overcrowded housing, congested streets, lack of playing space, polluted air, and so forth, which have harmful effects on the health, safety, and development of the children living there. Within such areas and cities there are some places where the depriviation of the children is aggravated by poverty.

To counteract these particular problems of children in the densely populated cities, the local authorities concerned provide various measures including the establishment of open-air schools and children's parks and playgrounds, in addition to those of the regular welfare services. Within the ordinary school programmes, emphasis is given to health education, safety education, and school meal service. In the rapidly developed areas there is a general shortage of school buildings and facilities, and special expansion projects have been undertaken by both the State and local authorities.

In 1970 the number of children of school age in the sparsely populated areas was estimated at some 600,000, 4·3 per cent of the total school population. They attended 7250 "remote area schools" which were mostly small schools with one or at best a few teachers. Thus the children in these areas suffered not only by their social and cultural isolation in daily life but also by the inferior education provided in such schools. It is commonly accepted that the children in the remote area schools are generally under-achieved and in an inferior physical condition.

One of the measures to improve this situation is the integration of small schools into one larger one, which naturally creates new problems of transportation and board of the children living in scattered villages or isolated islands. Thus, while the government encourages school integration with state subsidies under the Law Concerning Emergency Measures for the Sparsely Populated Areas of 1970, it assists local authorities under the Law for the Encouragement of Education in the Remote Areas of 1954 in the following ways: it provides buses or boats to transport children, it sets up boarding facilities, it assists with the costs for transportation and boarding, it sends doctors and dentists to the remote area schools, it appoints nursing teachers, it grants special allowances to the teachers, and it builds houses for them. The Ministry of Education also encourages the study of educational problems in these areas, and publishes the guidebooks for teachers working there.

Under the democratic Constitution efforts have been made to decrease various social prejudices against certain groups of people. There are at least four groups whose rights, including that of education, have been limited by such prejudices. The first group are women, whose social position in the long history of the nation has always been secondary to that of men. Thanks to the various social reforms after World War II, their social status has been much improved. In the field of education, the policies for co-education have provided them with an equal chance for education, and as far as the level of secondary education goes, the attendance rate of women has become nearly equal to that of men in the past decade.

In higher education, progress has been less remarkable. It is only within the past few years that the rate of college entrants among secondary school-leavers has become more balanced between the two sexes, and, as can be seen in Table 7 there is still a large difference between the number of those who attend college and those of the same age group. As is also shown in Table 8 a large part of the female student population attends two-year junior colleges, while those women in four-year colleges and graduate schools amount to a little over 20 per cent and less than 10 per cent respectively of the male students on the same levels. This inferior position of women in higher education evidently reflects the prejudice against women, particularly against their professional role in society, which is still prevalent and which may take some time to overcome.

Table 7

| | Percentage of students to age groups | | | | Percentage of college entrants to high school graduates | |
| | Secondary education | | Higher education | | | |
	Male	Female	Male	Female	Male	Female
1940	51·5	40·4	6·5	0·8		
1950	73·8	64·7	11·1	1·2	34·6	17·2
1955	81·6	74·3	14·5	3·1	20·9	14·9
1960	82·2	77·7	16·4	4·1	19·7	14·2
1965	85·1	82·5	22·8	7·4	30·1	20·4
1970	89·7	88·7	27·0	10·7	25·0	23·5

Table 8

| | Number of students, 1970 | |
	Male	Female
Junior colleges	44,784	214,963
Universities (undergraduates)	1,100,352	244,006
Graduate schools	37,381	3,576

The second group consists of some 2 million people who belong to the 4000–6000 of what are known as the "unemancipated communities". The origin of these communities goes back to the feudal period when Japanese society was stratified into several classes. At the time, the ancestors of this group of people constituted the outcast class, engaged in certain mean occupations and living in segregated communities. Although the feudal system of society was formally abolished by the Meiji Reform, the prejudice against these people still remained, and very little effort was made to improve their social status despite their ardent demand for equality. It has only been since the 1950s that the government has taken up this problem as a national policy. This is partly due to the democratic spirit of the time, but is due more to the rising self-consciousness of these people who formed a strong social movement for their emancipation.

The present policies of the government are based on the recommendations made by a prime minister's council on this problem in 1965, which include the following items: the improvement of living conditions such as housing, streets, water, and drainage; the improvement of social welfare services in community centres, health centres, nurseries, and children's clinics; technical and financial assistance to community work and the improvement of employment opportunities. For the children of the communities, efforts are to be made to bolster up academic abilities, to provide them with proper guidance, to offer them better health services and education, to secure regular attendance at school, and to ensure them the possibility of moving to higher stages of education. The teachers working in the schools which receive children from the communities will have favourable career prospects. The experimental projects in schools are to be encouraged and assisted. In order to raise the cultural and educational standards of the communities, school education must be supplemented by youth services and adult education. Parallel with these policies for assisting the children and adults in the "unemancipated communities",* measures must be taken to enlighten the general public on this problem.

Following these policy lines, various measures have been taken by both central and local governments. Each year the Ministry of Education has assigned a number of public schools to do experimental work in assisting the children of the "unemancipated communities". Since 1969 a group of pilot areas have been established to tackle this problem through joint efforts of the school and social education.

*They were often referred as *burakumin*, which literally meant the "residents of communities". Because of its discriminative connotation, the word is now avoided and is replaced by other terms such as the residents of "unemancipated communities" or *mikaiho-buraku*.

Japan is generally known as a mono-racial nation, but in fact it includes a few ethnic minority groups. The most famous of these is the Ainu, which in early times used to occupy the north-east part of the Japanese islands. However, owing to the exploitation of the superior Japanese and their century-long assimilation policy towards the Ainu, the latter has nearly disappeared as a pure ethnic group, although there are still a number of "Ainu communities" in the northern island, Hokkaido. As the population has been assimilated by the Japanese, the Ainu culture has died out, and except for a few isolated efforts no particular measures to preserve it have been taken, especially in the field of education.

Another ethnic minority is the Korean group, whose status in Japanese society is complicated by their past dependence on Japan and their present political division. There are some 600,000 Korean nationals in Japan, 30 per cent of whom immigrated or were forced to immigrate into Japan from Korea as cheap labour for the mean jobs during the colonial period, while the rest were second or third generation, born in Japan. Among the latter are some 150,000 children of school age.

One of the big problems for these Korean children is concerned with their national and cultural identity, which is not easy to preserve as they live in a Japanese society and are surrounded by its overwhelming culture. Furthermore, the Japanese harbour certain prejudices against them which has an unfavourable influence upon the cultivation of a proper national consciousness. To cope with this situation, the Korean communities maintain their own schools. As at 1967, some 34,000 children and young people attended 145 schools, including one college, which were recognized and supported by the government in North Korea, while some 2300 children went to twenty-one schools recognized by the government in South Korea. The majority of the Korean children, however, attend Japanese schools.

Another problem is the limited job opportunities for Korean young people. Despite the fact that they are well educated either through the Japanese school system or at the Korean schools, they find difficulty in getting jobs suited to their education and training because of their status as foreigners and because of the prejudices against them. This often results in a lack of learning motivation or in anti-social behaviour among some of the Korean young people.

HIGHER AND SOCIAL EDUCATION

Higher Education

In Japan, institutions for higher education include universities, junior colleges, and technical colleges. The School Education Law describes the aim of the university as being to teach and study higher learning as well as to give students broad general culture and intellectual, moral, and practical abilities. The junior college may lay emphasis on the training of abilities necessary for vocational or practical life. The technical college aims at teaching specialized arts as well as cultivating vocational abilities.

University and the junior college take students from among the graduates of the high school, providing for them four-year (six-year for medical and dental students) courses and two- to three-year courses respectively. The technical college, unlike the two other institutions, receives students from among the middle school graduates, offering them five-year courses.

The requirements for graduation from these three institutions are each prescribed in the university standards, the junior college standards, and the technical college standards and are as shown in Table 9.

Table 9

	Universities		Junior colleges		Technical colleges
			Courses		
	Four-year	Six-year	Two-year	Three-year	Five-year
	Credits[1]				Hours
General education	36	36	12	18	1785
Humanities	12	12	4	6	385
Natural sciences	12	12	4	6	980
Social sciences	12	12	4	6	420
Foreign languages	8	16			770
Physical education	4	4	2	3	350
Professional or specialized education	76	4000 hours	24	36	3640
Additional credits required		8	24	36	
Total	124	64 + 4000 hours	62	93	6545

[1]One credit requires one lecture class of one hour, one seminar class of two hours, and one laboratory work of three hours, each for the duration of fifteen weeks.

The university may establish graduate courses, the requirements of which are stipulated by the regulations concerning academic degrees. The masters degrees require two-years including thirty-credit course works and a thesis. The doctoral degrees require a five years of study, including fifty-credit course works and a thesis.

Table 10 shows the number of institutions for higher education and their students in 1970.

Table 10

	Universities	Graduate schools	Junior colleges	Technical colleges
Institutions				
State	75	59	22	49
Public	33	19	43	4
Private	274	102	414	7
Total	382	180	479	60
Students (in thousands)				
State	275	24	10	33
Public	46	2	16	4
Private	1024	15	234	7
Total	1345	41	260	44

The existing 382 universities may be divided into several groups in accordance with their history, aims, organization, and student bodies. The first group includes those which are called national "comprehensive" universities. They are the universities of Tokyo, Kyoto, Tohoku, Kyushu, Hokkaido, Osaka, Nagoya, and Hiroshima, and Tokyo University of Education, all of which are either former imperial universities or universities of arts and sciences, and which have distinguished themselves by the high quality of their learning.* They are composed of six to ten faculties and a varied number of research institutes. For example, Kyoto University consists of nine faculties of literature, education, law, economics, science, medicine, pharmacy, engineering, and agriculture, one division of liberal arts, and fourteen research institutes in arts and sciences both in basic and applied fields.

Some forty state "composite" universities form the second group. They were all set up by the 1949 reform on the basis of the single-faculty

*In October 1973 a new University of Tsukuba was founded, and Tokyo University of Education will be closed by 1977.

government universities, technical colleges, or normal schools. The "composite" university is usually small and is composed of a few faculties with the main emphasis on undergraduate education. Some of them, such as the universities of Kobe, Chiba, and a few others, have followed the lines of the "comprehensive" universities with several faculties offering postgraduate programmes as well as undergraduate ones. They are situated in the main cities of the prefectures, and usually serve as regional or local centres of higher learning. To this group also belong some half-dozen public, prefectural, or municipal universities.

The third group consists of some thirty state "single-faculty" universities, each of which is concentrated on one speciality or an area of higher learning. Some of them have a long history and have distinguished themselves in particular fields. Good examples are Hitotsubashi University in the social sciences, Tokyo Institute of Technology, Tokyo University of Foreign Languages, and Tokyo University of Fine Art and Music.

The fourth group includes 274 private universities which are further divided into "comprehensive", "composite", and "single-faculty" universities. Some twenty of them are "comprehensive", each of which consists of several faculties and research institutes and has a student population of over 10,000. They include such universities of secular foundation as Keio-Gijuku, Waseda, and Nihon, and those of Christian foundation such as Aoyama-Gakuin, Doshisha, Jochi, Kansei-Gakuin, and Rikkyo. Nihon University, the largest, has 11 faculties and 20 research institutes and a student population of some 64,000. Among the smaller ones are such universities as the International Christian University, Tamagawa, the Buddhist Taisho and Koyasan, and a group of women's universities, which have distinguished themselves by their unique history and the quality of their education.

The fifth group consists of 83 women's universities, (2 state, 6 public, and 75 private). The majority of them offer courses in liberal arts and home economics but some are specialized in such professional education as medicine and pharmacy. Among them, such women's universities as the state Ochanomizu and Nara and the private Nihon, Tsuda-Juku, Tokyo, and Tokyo Medical, have achieved fame by their pioneer role in women's higher education.

To the last group belong 8 state universities of education or teacher-training universities and 38 faculties of education or teacher-training faculties, each of which is part of the state "composite" university. Each of these 46 teacher education institutions is situated in one of the 46 prefectures and functions primarily to provide teachers for public elementary and middle schools in the prefecture concerned. Some private universities also train elementary school teachers, and the majority of high school teachers and a large number of middle school teachers are trained in faculties other than education in the state universities as well as in the public and private ones. The eight national "comprehensive" universities (Osaka excepted) have faculties of education which, unlike those mentioned above, are primarily specialized in research and training in educational science.

The majority of the 479 junior colleges are small in size, consisting of one to three departments or courses in one related area, with a student population of a few hundred. Only a few provide a variety of courses from liberal arts to engineering, with the students exceeding 1000. In 1970 these 479 junior colleges offered 1127 courses, among which 75 per cent were in the areas of domestic sciences, liberal arts, teacher training for kindergartens and day-nurseries, and fine arts, while the rest were in commerce and business studies, engineering, agriculture, and para-medical preparation. This indicates that the major function of the Japanese junior colleges is in women's higher education followed by semi-professional training for both women and men.

The opportunities for part-time and correspondence course education are provided in both the university and junior college. In 1970 some 50 universities and 100 junior colleges offered part-time courses. The graduation requirements are the same as those for full-time students, but the duration of the courses is usually one year longer than that of full-time courses. The percentage of part-time students in the total student body was 10 per cent in the universities and 14 per cent in the junior colleges. In the same year 11 universities and 7 junior colleges offered correspondence courses, and the number of those registered in the courses was equivalent to 5 and 8 per cent of the student population of the universities and junior colleges respectively.

Social Education

People may seek after opportunities for education outside the regular school system for different personal reasons, which, roughly speaking, can be classified into either professional or cultural. In Japan, such opportunities for professional purposes are provided mainly in the training institutions within industry or in the so-called "miscellaneous schools". The opportunities for cultural education are provided mainly by the public "facilities for social education" and by the voluntary "social education organizations". There are cases, however, in which the institutions within industry and the miscellaneous schools offer cultural education, while the social education facilities provide professional training.

Industrial training is provided under the Industrial Training Law of 1958 (revised in 1969) by public industrial training centres and by centres set up by enterprises or corporations. The training aims to produce skilled labourers, to maintain and improve their skills, or to re-train them. In 1969 there were 419 public training centres with 124,000 trainees and 59,927 authorized non-public centres with 84,000 trainees. There are 185 kinds of training prescribed by the Law, and the duration of the training courses varies from one to three years. The training course includes not only the theory and practice of the specific job, but also some elements of general education. The attempts to combine industrial training with part-time high school education have been referred to already in the previous chapter.

Apart from industrial training under the Law, it is common for large enterprises to provide their own training schemes, either for newly recruited employees, or for workers engaged in new technical fields or top or middle level management. The opportunities for cultural education are also often provided by the enterprises or by labour unions.

The educational establishments which are not classified as institutions for elementary, secondary, and higher education are collectively called "miscellaneous schools". They include all sorts of schools differing from each other in size, organization, curriculum, teaching staff, student body, etc. Quite a number of them are almost equivalent to junior colleges in the quality of the education, while others offer a limited level of practical training. The majority provide young people with vocational and practical education in such fields as dressmaking and home economics, bookkeeping, typing, mechanics, hairdressing, nursing and other para-medical techniques, kindergarten and nursery teaching, fine arts, etc. Some offer courses in liberal arts and foreign languages. As of 1970 there were some 8000 miscellaneous schools with a total enrolment of 1,353,000.

The "facilities for social education" are provided either by the public (state or local) authorities or by voluntary efforts. The kind and number of social education facilities in 1970 are shown in Table 11.

Table 11

	State	Local	Private	Total
Citizens' public halls		13,785		13,785[1]
Libraries	4	695	29	728[1]
Museums	28	150	160	338[1]
Audio-visual libraries		499	380	879[1]
Youth houses	7	175		182
Children's cultural centres		28		28
Children's nature centres		4		4
Women's halls		12	35	47
Public facilities for physical education and recreation		1,781		1,781

[1] In 1968.

The function of the citizens' public hall is prescribed by the Social Education Law as being to provide the people in the community with a variety of educational and cultural activities, to improve their intellectual, cultural, and physical life, and thus to increase the welfare of the community. As of 1970, over 90 per cent of the municipalities had established citizens' public halls. The activities offered include courses, lectures and meetings on educational and cultural topics for young people, adults, women, parents, and aged people, and gatherings for recreation and physical education.

The "youth house" aims at providing young people with an opportunity for residential group training by offering a variety of short-term training courses and by accommodating them with residential facilities for their own activities. In 1968 the seven state youth houses received a total of 630,000 trainees, among which 54 per cent were working youth, 30 per cent were students, and the rest included youth leaders and others. The local youth houses offer similar opportunities as the state ones. In 1968 they accommodated more than 1,890,000 young people.

The voluntary "social education organizations" include various kinds of groups which are engaged in activities for social education on the local as well as national level. They provide their members with a variety of educational, cultural, and recreational opportunities either by themselves, or in co-operation with the public social education facilities. There are some twenty national youth organizations including the YMCA, the YWCA, the Japan Four-H Club Association, the Japan Youth Unesco Association, etc. The largest of them is the Japanese Council for Youth Organizations with some 1,500,000 members, which is the federation of the large number of community youth organizations. Some other groups, such as the Boy Scouts and Girl Guides, the National Federation of Children's Clubs, and a half-dozen other national organizations are concerned with out-of-school education for younger children. There are also some half-dozen national women's organizations, such as the National Society for Women's Social Education, the University Women's Association, and others. The largest of these is the National Council for the Community Women's Organization with some 20,000 member organizations and a total membership of 6,300,000.

Table 12

	Courses	Participants
Youth classes	4,131	200,609
Women's classes	50,441	2,407,213
Home education classes	14,903	1,084,315
Adult classes	21,934	1,253,450 (1968)
Extension services	121	9,405
Universities	47	4,930
Junior colleges	9	570
Senior high schools	65	3,905
Correspondence courses	148	710,348 (1969)

The Parent–Teacher Associations (PTA) are also active in the field of social education. The purpose of the PTA is to assist the proper development of young children and young people in and out of school with the joint efforts of parents and teachers, by improving the environmental conditions for children and youths, by providing appropriate care for them and by encouraging parents and teachers towards self-improvement. The idea of the PTA was originally introduced during the occupation period, and spread nationwide in a relatively short period. According to the survey conducted in 1962 there were 45,000 PTAs with a total membership of 1,770,000, nearly 30 per cent of the adult population of Japan. In the same year, 36,000 PTAs organized adult education courses or meetings for their members with a total of 1,900,000 participants.

A variety of courses for young people and adults are organized by social education facilities and voluntary organizations. In addition, extension service courses are provided by the schools and universities. Opportunities for social education are also given by correspondence courses offered by the public and private institutions. The kind and number of such courses and the numbers of participants in 1970 are shown in Table 12.

CHAPTER 8

Japanese Education for the 1970s

In 1969 Japan observed the centenary of the foundation of its modern government, which caused much reflection on its past achievement and future prospects with regard to various aspects of the nation's life, including education. Reflecting the internal and external condition in which Japan found itself at the time, the general tone of the thinking was a mixture of complacency and criticism, although understandably the government side tended to be optimistic while the opposition was less optimistic and more critical.

Japan had made the most remarkable progress in the past century and particularly in the last twenty years in the field of economics and industry, which enabled the standard of living and welfare of the people to be raised to a level that they had never enjoyed before. On the other hand, the over-hasty tempo of economic progress had caused certain kinds of destruction and maladjustment, both in the physical environment and in the mental and cultural life of the people.

Politically, Japan had been relatively stable for the last century, and the democratic forms of government which had been adopted since 1946 appeared to have taken root. On the other hand, twenty years' continuous dominance by the conservatives had sometimes made the parliamentary process merely perfunctory and had tended to alienate the opposition from the government, often resulting in political irresponsibility on both sides.

Viewed internationally, Japan's progress over the century had been motivated mainly by its desire to catch up with advanced nations. Although certain serious mistakes had occurred, this had worked well on the whole as long as Japan was able to find the models to follow. After a century of striving, Japan suddenly realized to its perplexity that there

150

would be no more models for its further development, and that it should seek new relationships with other nations, both developed and developing.

In the field of national education, the Minister of Education took the initiative in such thinking, first by referring to the Central Council for Education in 1967 the topic "fundamental policies and measures for the future expansion and development of school education" for their deliberation. The Council submitted two interim reports in 1969 and 1970 and a final one in 1971. The Minister of Education also asked the Council for Social Education in 1968 to consider "policies for social education to meet the radical changes in social structures". The Council's report was made in 1971. In 1970 the Ministry of Education published its White Paper entitled *Educational Standards in Japan* to publicize the achievements of Japanese education in a comparative perspective. Commemorating the centenary of the promulgation of the Fundamental Code of Education (1872), the Ministry in 1972 also published a 1900 page chronicle, *A Hundred Years of the National System of Education*, which reviewed the development of national education over the century with the intention of providing historical justification for the present Ministry's policies.

These documents, and in particular the reports of the Central Council for Education, stimulated public interest in the matter and raised considerable controversy in educational circles. To emulate such government actions, in 1970 the Japan Teachers' Union (JTU), the strongest rival to the Ministry of Education, set up a Commission for Inquiry into the Educational System, which published its first report in 1971, its second in 1972, and its third in 1973. While many other organizations expressed their opinions, both pro and con, on the Ministry's policy documents in this period, the reports of the JTU were the strongest and most comprehensive criticisms of the Ministry.

Around this time there also occurred an interesting incident, when the Organization for Economic Co-operation and Development (OECD) reviewed educational policy and planning in Japan by appointing examiners* and holding a "confrontation meeting" with the representatives of the Japanese government in 1970. The report of the meeting, together with

*The examiners were Joseph Ben-David, Israel; Ronald P. Dore, United Kingdom; Johan Galtung, Norway; Edgar Faure, France; Edwin Reischauer, United States; and Bersford Hayward, OECD.

the examiners' reports, was published by the OECD as *Reviews of National Policies for Education: Japan* in 1971. This OECD action brought into the controversy an international standpoint on the problems of national education, and made the Japanese realize that the answers to these questions should be of relevance not only nationally but also internationally.

The reports of the three organizations mentioned above, i.e. the Ministry of Education, the JTU, and the OECD covered (with different emphasis naturally) the major points of the problems which Japanese national education was facing and would be required to solve in the 1970s. The following chapter therefore will attempt to examine some of the major problems of Japanese national education in the 1970s by reviewing the arguments put forward by these reports.

DIFFERENT APPROACHES TO THE REFORM

Among both government and opposition circles there was a general feeling of dissatisfaction, or even a sense of crisis, with the present status of the national education. This discontent, however, seemed to stem from different views of the present situation. The government took the position that the present crisis in national education was caused mainly by the gap between existing school education and changing society, while the opposition saw the major source of the problems in the inflexible centralization policy which failed to meet the varying educational demands of the people.

The different standpoint of these opposing forces can be seen in their attitudes toward the educational reforms after World War II. The government, following the Central Council for Education, named the proposals made by the latter as those for the "Third Educational Reform", implying the epoch-making nature of the proposed reform which might match in significance the first reform in 1872 and the second one in 1947.

According to the official interpretation of the Ministry of Education, the first and second reforms, which laid down foundations for national education and democratic education respectively, were both undertaken as part of political programmes that Japan (under strong external pressure) was forced to set up. Both reforms also adopted the foreign system of education of the advanced countries as their models, and were carried out in unfavourable economic situations which made full realization of the reform plans difficult. These conditions in the first and second reforms necessitated subsequent modifications and readjustments. With regard to the 1947 reform, various measures had been taken to readjust the original programmes in the following twenty years, and it was now time to make an overall examination of the consequence of the reform and to propose new educational plans which should meet the demand of the time.

In opposition to the government's attitude toward the 1947 Reform, the JTU and their allies considered the proposed programmes of the 1947 reform to be fundamentally correct and still relevant, and to have the full support of the majority of the people. From this point of view the government's measures for readjusting the original programmes were all looked on with suspicion, with the idea that they might twist the basic spirit of this democratic reform, and that what the government ought to do was not to make any overall changes in the 1947 reform plans but to make every effort to fully realize them.

A corresponding difference existed in the two parties' methods of approaching the problems. As has been observed in an earlier chapter, the government regarded the decentralization of educational administration as one of the difficulties in the 1947 Reform, and took various measures towards centralization or re-centralization over twenty years. In pushing the Third Educational Reform, the government made it clear that the Reform should be carried out under its initiative. It is true that the Central Council for Education suggested some of the major proposals, such as the reorganization of the school system on an experimental basis, and sought the co-operation of schools, universities, and other organizations concerned in carrying out the reform plans. On the other hand, the Council, by clarifying the positive role of the government, gave a general impression that the leading reformer should be the government.

The proposed leadership by the government caused a strong reaction from the opposition. The JTU, in opposition to government monopoly in policymaking, maintained that the reform should be made on a broader basis, i.e. the people, including above all parents and teachers, and by suggesting the further decentralization of power and the greater freedom of teachers, proposed that the initiative for educational reform should be given into the hands of the local population and the teaching profession.

The opponents pointed out that, while the Central Council mentioned the necessity of seeking the co-operation of other bodies, no specific mention was made of the latter's role in the reform, making a sharp contrast with its positive remarks on the government's leadership. It is fair to say that before making its final report the Council invited, through public hearings and other opportunities, the comments and suggestions from various organizations and individuals, including those representing the local population and the teaching profession. It is true, however, that the Council itself was represented in its membership only by those in sympathy with or neutral to the government, and not by those holding the opposite point of view.

As observed in earlier chapters, the opposition of the two parties, represented respectively by the Ministry of Education and the JTU, was an old story in the post-World-War-II development of Japanese education. The examiners of the OECD were impressed among other things by the sharp polarization of the most articulate groups in education, a situation which existed even in the teaching profession, and by the blockage in communication between groups at different levels of authority and even between those at parallel levels. The examiners felt that such tendencies seemed to have been reinforced and would be accelerated further by the policy of centralization of power that the Japanese government had been taking. The centralization would also stifle educational creativity and innovation.

In reply the representatives of the Japanese government maintained that the purpose of its central control was to ensure a minimum and universal quality in school education and that, therefore, beyond that level, schools and teachers were given a great deal of freedom to experiment and innovate. To improve communication, both sides would have to exert themselves, and as long as the anti-government prejudice of certain groups remained, it would be difficult to open the blockage despite all the government's efforts. The inclusion of representatives with conflicting views, as suggested by the examiners, was hard to adopt immediately because of the present political climate with its sharp polarization of opinions. The centralized power of the Ministry of Education, they felt, should be seen in the historical context of the modernization of Japan, in which the government exercised strong leadership.

The last remark presented a typical example of the position of the government, which made the proposals for the Third Educational Reform on the same lines as Japan had taken under the government's leadership in modernization during the century. The traditional pattern of governance in education was thus taken for granted, and the decentralization of power under the Second Educational Reform after World War II was regarded as an episode. Therefore, despite various new suggestions made by it, the proposed Third Educational Reform was fundamentally of a conservative nature.

On the other hand, the opposition, represented by the JTU, appeared to be less progressive by their rejection of the proposed changes and by their sticking to the existing system. For them, however, the existing system was basically an outcome of the Second Educational Reform which was the antithesis of pre-World-War-II Japanese education. Therefore, sticking to the existing system meant for them making fundamental changes in the traditional forms and governance of national education. In this sense, the position of the opposition was radical and had things in common with that of the OECD examiners to some extent.

IMPROVEMENT OF EDUCATION IN QUANTITY AND QUALITY

The necessity of the further improvement of the elementary and secondary stages of national education, both in quantity and in quality, was agreed on by all parties who, however, made different suggestions according to their own views. In proposing the expansion of educational opportunities, the Central Council for Education pointed out two priority areas, i.e. pre-school education and special education. It set up as an immediate target the universal attendance at kindergarten of five-year-old children, and suggested greater public financial assistance to the municipalities and private kindergartens, to expand the number of places, and, particularly in the latter cases, to ease the financial burden of the parents. It also considered the possibility of setting up a new type of "infant school" which should provide four years' continuous education for children aged between 4 and 7.

To expand educational opportunities for the physically and mentally handicapped, the adoption of the compulsory attendance at nursing schools, which had been postponed, was made an immediate goal by the Council. The establishment of nursing schools should be made obligatory for all municipalities, and different forms of education, including visiting teachers, should be developed according to the various needs of the handicapped children. The State should take a more positive role in this field, e.g. by means of establishing special schools for the children with dual handicaps.

While there was general support in choosing the above two areas for the priority list, some groups, represented by the JTU, suggested adding another area, i.e. high school education, and criticized the Council for this omission. Although the Central Council had not failed to realize the possible increase in high school enrolment, which, according to its estimate, would reach a level of 96 per cent in ten years, it did not make any positive suggestions to guarantee such attendance, particularly for those in difficulty, except in general terms, such as the improvement of the study-work conditions of the part-time students.

The JTU, in proposing the idea of high school education as a right of young people, suggested the expansion of facilities in public high schools and financial assistance to private high schools. The high schools which charged tuition (both public and private) should be made free, with increasing public financial support. Measures should be taken to encourage part-time high school education for working youths and to improve special education at this level for the physically and mentally handicapped. As a model for high schools, the union advocated "comprehensive community high schools" which challenged the "diversified high schools" of the government, as will be seen later.

To improve the quality of education, the Central Council made several proposals on the grounds of its analysis of the defects in the existing system, such as: over-extensive curricula at an early stage where basic education should be emphasized; duplication and inconsistency in curricula of schools at different stages; neglect of individual differences at the high school level. To meet such defects it suggested first a re-examination of the curricula content and the development of new curricula so that basic education could be secured at elementary schools, and that continuity and consistency could be maintained throughout all stages of schooling. Diversification of the content of high school curricula was also proposed to enable students to choose courses suited to their particular abilities and interests. The courses should be flexible enough to make it easy for individual students to transfer from one course to another, according to the development of their abilities and change of interest. In this connection, the student guidance should be improved and better organized.

To ensure the efficiency of teaching at all levels, further studies should be made on various measures, which could be adopted to individual needs, while ensuring the attainment of the common educational objectives. The Central Council made special mention of the following items: flexible class management by employing techniques like group instruction, individualized teaching and learning, non-graded school, and advanced placement.

The Council further proposed the development of a new school system in place of the existing one and for the gradual implementation of the reform, suggested the setting up of a series of experimental pilot projects which should cover the following points: the establishment of "infant schools" which would provide children between 4 and 7 with the kind of education suitable for them; the amalgamation of the existing middle school and high school into a secondary school with six years' continuous education which would avoid the overlapping in the curricula of the existing two schools; the formation of new school ladders with a different articulation, such as 4–4–6, 4–5–5, or 6–6, as opposed to the existing 6–3–3, and the application to other types of educational institutions of the five-year course already established in existing technical colleges, which covered the stages of education at high school and junior college levels.

A variety of opinions, both pro and con, were expressed about these proposals of the Central Council. There was general agreement on the defects of the existing system which the Council pointed out, but again there were different approaches to the problems. For example, the JTU also suggested a drastic cut in the curricula content and the inclusion and increase of elective subjects in the curricula at all levels. However, it criticized the Council's omission of the questions on high school selection, which, together with the college selection, affected the curricula of lower schools and caused such problems as the over-extensiveness of the curricula. It also criticized the diversification of the high school curricula into various specialities, pointing out that it was designed to meet the demands of industrial circles and would not meet the real needs of the students who suffered from discrimination among the courses of different specialities and from a resulting severe competition in selection. The JTU proposed the idea of "comprehensive community high schools" which would take in all youths in a community, providing them with a common social experience as well as a variety of subject-matter on the obligatory and elective bases.

As observed in earlier chapters, the opposition between the Council and the JTU on the high school curricula was not a new story, and stemmed from the difference in their philosophies of education and society, which were often conventionally called, respectively, selectionist and egalitarian. The selectionistic view of the government was also criticized by the OECD examiners who questioned whether an emphasis on selection rather than on the development of the innate abilities of students did not take place at practically all levels of education in the Japanese school system. In reply, the Ministry of Education, while admitting certain defects in the system, pointed out that the emphasis on selection was associated with the desire of the Japanese people to advance, and with their competitiveness, which had been the cause of Japan's progress over a century.

There was a truism in the remark of the Ministry. The selectionism was closely related to the nature of Japanese society and, through its historical development had become almost innate in the Japanese system of education. Here again the conservatism of the government could be observed, and a challenge to it lay in the egalitarianism of the opposition. On the other hand, the latter found difficulty in fully convincing the general public of its ideas, which, because of the wide gap between them and reality, still sounded too idealistic.

TEACHERS

No change in education is possible unless teachers are prepared for it. The Central Council thus made several proposals to improve the preparation and the status of teachers. For the initial training of teachers, the existing system should be strengthened by the State's initiative in improving facilities and teaching conditions at the state colleges (or universities) of education for elementary and secondary teachers and in levelling up the standards for the qualifications of secondary teachers to be trained in other universities.

To guarantee the qualities of the newly recruited teachers, a year of probation should be better organized by the employing authorities. Institutions of graduate school status should be established for the in-service training of teachers as well as for the advanced study of education, and those who received training there should be given a special qualification as specialized teachers and a correspondingly higher status and salary. In general, the teachers' salary should be much improved so as to attract qualified individuals into the profession.

Finally, it was suggested that teachers should exert themselves to improve in quality through their own professional organizations, and to earn the respect and trust of society which would recognize teachers as professionals who require highly specialized skills and knowledge and with a professional standard of ethics. The professional organizations of teachers should be neutral and refrain from any political activities.

No-one disagreed with the Council on the necessity of improving the quality of teachers, but the proposed initiative of the State aroused strong reaction from the opposition side. The JTU opposed the idea of separate state institutions for teacher training, which, for its mind, meant the return to the old "normal school" tradition. Such institutions would be readily subject to state control and would remain as "second citizens" in higher education. It advocated that training both for elementary and secondary teachers should take place within universities. The in-service training of teachers should not be organized for the convenience of the administration or for the control of teachers, but should be considered as a right of teachers.

The JTU most strongly opposed the proposed creation of a rank of specialist teachers, considering it a step towards advancing the bureaucracy of hierarchical order in the teaching profession, and also a means for the "divide-and-rule" policy against the profession. It also considered the Council's comment on the political neutrality of the teachers' organizations a challenge to their freedom, and responded that the government, under the name of political neutrality, intended to control teachers under its own political ideology.

The OECD examiners rightly pointed out the difficulty of the questions on political neutrality in education in a country such as Japan where polarization of political opinions was so great and a single party had a long-standing monopoly of power. In such a case both the government and the opposition tended to see education in terms of its potential for political indoctrination.

The question of the political neutrality of the teaching profession was thus closely linked with the general political situation in Japan. As observed earlier, the Ministry of Education and the JTU had long been in confrontation about the questions not only directly related with the status of teachers, but also concerning various government policies in education. The government was suspicious that the JTU would exert its political influence over children through its member teachers, and repeated its position that ideological doctrines should not be brought into the classroom whatever the conviction of a teacher or a union. In connection with the examiners' comment on the reform of local administration in 1956, the Ministry also indicated its objection to the political participation of the JTU, saying that the dominance of the unions over the popularly elected boards of education necessitated the reform of the appointed boards.

The JTU, for its part, was convinced that the Ministry had developed the policies towards its own political orientation and intended to influence the children through classroom teachers, and that the Ministry thus planned not only to exclude the JTU from policy formation in education but also to divert the JTU's influence over individual teachers. The JTU was also afraid that, with the diminishing power of the union, the rights of individual teachers as citizens and professionals would be endangered.

Thus, as the OECD examiners pointed out, the communication gap between the opposing sides was deep and seemed to be further widened by the issue on the nature of the teaching profession.

HIGHER EDUCATION

The Central Council for Education estimated that in the ten years between 1970 and 1980 the numbers of students entering the universities and the junior colleges would increase respectively from 17·1 to 31·9 per cent and from 6·5 to 15·3 per cent of the given age groups. Higher education in the 1970s must thus be able to accommodate this great increase in the student population with their diversified educational needs while securing higher academic standards in research and teaching. To meet these demands, the Council designed a model of higher education which was to consist of five types of institutions with objectives, curricula, and student bodies different from each other.

The five types of higher institution were: (1) the universities with three- to four-year courses, which could be general, specialized, or vocationally oriented: (2) the junior colleges with two-year general or vocational courses: (3) the technical colleges with five-year courses following middle school education: (4) the graduate schools with two- to three-year courses for advanced specialized training or for in-service or recurrent education of mature students: and (5) the institutes for higher learning providing the advanced students with the opportunities for research and training at the doctoral level.

The programmes for general education should be improved in (1) and (2), while measures should be taken to secure research activities in (4) and (5). The methods of instruction should be improved in all institutions. The improvement in the procedures of selecting students was also necessary.

As for the university administration, the Council proposed the establishment of a central administrative machinery within a university, consisting of the president, the vice-presidents, and those appointed both inside and outside the university, and the division of functions between this administrative body and the faculty senates or meetings. Such centralized administrative power would respond more to the varied needs and demands of society as well as of the students, in comparison with the existing one which was decentralized and scattered among the constituent faculties.

To improve the quality of teaching and research, the Council emphasized the necessity of general improvement of the working conditions of teaching and research staff. It also suggested that the present tenure system might be replaced by one of a definite-term contract, so that personnel mobility would be more secure in accordance with the needs of the institutions and the abilities of individuals.

The Council observed that the further development of higher education would require state financial aid to a considerable extent, and that, in particular, assistance should be given on a larger scale to the private universities and colleges which had been, and would be, accommodating the majority of the student population. To secure the effective use of its resources, the government should develop a long-range plan for the overall capacity of higher education the types of higher education in relation to purposes, curricular, and student bodies, the enrolments in different fields of specialization, and the balanced regional distribution of higher institutions.

As mentioned earlier, these recommendations of the Central Council were primarily based on its anticipation of the growing demands for the expansion of higher education in the 1970s. In the process of deliberation, however, the Council also had to concern itself with the immediate problems which arose during the nationwide campus unrest in 1968 and

1969. The unrest, which spread through 40 per cent of the universities of the country, varied in direct cause and form, but everywhere it revealed in the most dramatic way the problems of higher education to the general public and to those directly concerned with education. Thus the university problem became a national issue and was hotly debated in different quarters of society. According to a survey, some 400 proposals were made public on this issue in this period, out of which nearly 90 per cent were made from within the universities themselves.

In November 1968 the Minister of Education asked the Central Council for Education to consider "measures to meet the university problems on hand". The Council, which had already been deliberating the question of higher education in accordance with the previous request of the Minister in July 1967, responded quickly, submitting a report in April of the following year. While the report admitted that the problems on the campus should be understood within the broader context of political and social unrest, it was critical of the traditional forms of university administration which failed to meet the changes occurring both inside and outside the universities.

Based on the recommendations made by the Council's report, the government drew up a Bill for Emergency Measures of University Administration, which became a law in August 1969. The law made clear the responsibility of the university and its administration to solve the troubles on the campus, and gave the president of the university, if the occasion demanded, certain powers to centralize his authority by means of appointing his executives and an advisory council which could supersede part or whole of the authority of the faculties. The law also provided the Minister of Education with the powers to ask for the submission of a report from the university in trouble, to make his recommendations on it, to suspend its educational and research functions, and to appoint an Extraordinary Council on University problems, an advisory body to the Minister, which would mediate in the troubled university.

This emergency law understandably excited strong reaction from the opposition sides, universities, and student organizations, who supported the traditional autonomy of the university and its faculties. The law, however, functioned as a kind of trump card for the government, and by the beginning of 1970 the nationwide campus unrest calmed down, although the law was never applied.

The Central Council, for its part, continued its deliberation on higher education and, when it made its final report in June 1971, the ideas which it had formulated in its report of 1968 constituted an important part. And it was this part that invited the strongest objection, above all from among the universities.

The Association of State Universities, for example, questioned the proposed centralization of university administration and the leadership of the government in university reform, although it did not deny the necessity for the reform. Instead it favoured the faculty-oriented administration and university reform based on the autonomous and voluntary efforts of individual universities. The Private Universities Association also objected to the government's leadership in university reform and held its position for the freedom and initiative of individual private universities in this matter, while agreeing with certain parts of the Council's suggestion.

Here again there was sharp opposition between two claims – the government's leadership and the university autonomy. At the time when the campus troubles appeared to have been solved only by the strong stand of the government, the claim for university autonomy might sound hopeless. Despite hundreds of reform proposals made during the period of trouble from within the universities, little progress was made in the early 1970s for the reform of the universities on their own initiative. On the other hand, no university reform was possible for the government without voluntary co-operation of the universities, who claimed autonomy. Furthermore, among the latter there was a criticism of the government that the existing laws and regulations, maintaining uniformity and conformity, were obstacles to the internal reforms of the universities and that the government, while encouraging the changes on the government line, did not give full support to the innovations in other directions.

In relation to this last point, the question of student participation in the university administration should be mentioned. It was one of the major items about which the students made demands during the campus unrest, and a number of the proposals for university reform made from within the universities took a positive attitude towards the expansion of those areas in which the students should participate. On the other hand, there were a number of opinions, both inside and outside academic circles, which expressed doubt on unlimited student participation. The Central

Council admitted the necessity of hearing the voices of students on such matters as curricula and student welfare services, but denied their direct participation in university administration including personnel matters, finance, and evaluation of the students' work. During and after the period of campus unrest, there were several cases when the appointment of the president or the deal of a faculty in the state university was rejected by the Ministry of Education on the grounds that the students participated in the election. In such cases, the Ministry clearly discouraged the measure which was innovated by the university, but in the direction which was opposite to that taken by the government.

The question of university entrance was mentioned by all as one of the most serious problems in Japanese higher education, and a number of suggestions were made to improve the situation. It was generally agreed, however, that the problem was so complicated and deeply rooted in Japanese society that no single answer could be found. Another question was university finance, which will be discussed in the following section, together with the question of educational finance as a whole.

PLANNING, IMPLEMENTING, AND FINANCING THE EDUCATIONAL REFORM

The Central Council for Education proposed in its report the basic policies which should be taken by the government to implement its recommendations. Firstly, the government should introduce the reform of elementary and secondary education progressively, learning from the experimental pilot projects. In implementing the pilot projects, the government should establish a system by which co-operation among the State, local authorities, and individual schools could be secured to achieve the goals. The government should also ensure the co-operation of researchers, educators, and administrators in the research and development which would serve as a basis for the reform.

Taking into consideration the fact that the quality of teachers was the most important factor in determining the quality of education, the government should take all necessary measures to improve the training and the status of teachers. As to higher education, the government should set up a national plan, establish new institutions, and improve existing ones progressively. The government should seek co-operation with existing universities and colleges. It should introduce legal changes necessary to rationalize the internal administration of the state universities.

To guarantee equal opportunities for education suited to the abilities of all, the government should take drastic steps to improve the scholarship system, ensuring an equal geographical distribution of educational institutions and subsidizing private schools and universities. The government should promote the diversification of the content of education at school levels beyond compulsory education so as to provide effective education suited to individual differences. The reform of the admission procedures of universities should be promoted by the government in co-operation with the universities.

On receiving the Council's report in June 1971, the Ministry of Education launched preparations for the reform, firstly by the immediate establishment of an office for educational reform headed by the Vice-Minister of Education. In the following months various government efforts to implement the recommendations of the Central Council could be observed.

Early in 1972, a Section for Research and Development was established within the Ministry, through which the school reform was to be studied and planned. By the end of the year, the Ministry had commissioned twenty-two groups of teachers and researchers to make studies on topics related to the proposed pilot projects. The immediate establishment of "infant schools" was postponed because of strong opposition, but experimental researches related to this new type of school were included in the above studies. Meanwhile the Ministry increased the state subsidy to expand kindergarten education. In November 1973 the Minister referred the Curriculum Council to examine the curricula of elementary, middle, and high schools with a view to continuation and integration among them.

For the training of teachers, the Council on Teacher Training made its report in July 1972 on the lines of the recommendations of the Central Council. The report suggested that to raise the professional standards of teachers the requirements for teachers certificates should be tightened in the professional and pedagogical subjects, including the prolongation of the period of teaching practice, and suggested that the training of kindergarten and elementary school teachers should be undertaken in principle by the state teacher-training institutions. The changes in the regulations for teachers certificates were left pending, but the expansion of teacher training in the state institutions was envisaged. In addition to the expansion of the existing state teachers colleges, the Ministry planned to

set up by 1976 at least two state teachers colleges with graduate programmes in May 1973 and appointed a Committee for the Study of the
New Teacher Training Colleges and Graduate Schools.

As to higher education, in June 1972, the Minister of Education
appointed a Conference on Higher Education, which was to make plans for
expansion in view of the recommendations made by the Central Council.
In its first report of March 1973, the conference pointed out that by the
middle of the 1980s a further expansion of higher education would be
required to meet the ever-increasing student population, which would
reach 40 per cent. It set up a few guidelines for expansion. Firstly, to
avoid the centralization of higher institutions in large cities and
metropolises, encouragement should be given to the establishment of new
local universities and colleges as well as to the expansion of the existing
local ones. Secondly, prefectural and municipal institutions should play an
important role in such localization of higher education. Thirdly, as the
expansion would still depend on private efforts, the state subsidy should
be enlarged to maintain private universities, and colleges.

The conference should also discuss detailed plans on a university of the
air, new teacher-training colleges, new technical and para-medical colleges,
and other new types of higher institutions, all of which the Ministry of
Education intended to establish in the latter half of the 1970s.

For state assistance to private schools and universities, in November
1973 the Ministry set up a Conference on "Measures to Encourage Private
Schools and Universities", which was to examine the basic questions of
state administration over private institutions and of the state assistance to
them. In 1970 the Ministry had started a five-year plan to assist with part
of the maintenance cost of private universities including personnel costs,
and by 1974 the state subsidy should cover some 10 per cent of the total
maintenance cost. As is generally agreed, this was entirely insufficient to
meet the increasing cost, and in order to reduce the burden on parents and
to bring up the quality of education to the level of the state universities,
further expansion of state assistance was required. On the other hand,
through the state subsidy, a new relationship had been developing between
the government and private institutions, and among the latter group there
existed anxiety about the possible extension of state control over them.

Throughout the implementation of these measures taken in the early
1970s, the government's leadership seems to have been clearly established

to the extent that this "Third Educational Reform" might be critically called "government oriented". It is true that the government has to a certain extent secured the co-operation of other bodies concerned, i.e. the local authorities, universities, and teachers. Although the opposition parties are having more influence in certain local areas, local government as a whole is still under the strong hold of the central government. The national associations of local boards of education and of superintendents earlier expressed their agreement on the proposed reform, and some local authorities, though small in number, have been co-operating in the pilot projects. While its national association keeps a critical position on the Central Council's recommendation, some of the state universities have been developing their reform plans on similar lines to those which the Council proposed. The Ministry also seems to have ensured the co-operation of teachers of non-JTU sects.

On the other hand, it is equally true that the reform still lacks wide national support and that its progress has been hindered by the old antagonism and partisanship in the nation. It can even be said that the proposed reform has accelerated opposition, and further deepened the gap already existing among the people. A good example of the sterility of such antagonism is the issue of teachers' salaries. The government, in accordance with the recommendation of the Central Council, planned a general raise in the salary scales of teachers but failed to pass the related bill through the National Diet because of strong objection by the opposition. The JTU, which was behind the opposition, was suspicious that the proposed salary raise, accompanied by a new grading system, would be utilized by the government as an effective tool to divide and control the teachers. Thus, despite general agreement about raising the teachers' salaries, the issue is still pending today.*

This is only one of many other cases in which the lack of co-operation has made itself a hindrance to the progress of reform. As the OECD examiners said, the filling of the communications gap among those concerned is one of the most important keys for the further development of Japanese education.

In the last part of the report, the Central Council made estimates of the cost necessary for expansion and innovation in the coming ten years.

*In March 1974 a bill for improving teachers' salaries finally passed the National Diet.

The Council first estimated the increased enrolment between 1970 and 1980 as 14·0 per cent in compulsory education, 17·0 per cent in high schools, 88·0 per cent in junior colleges, and 49·0 per cent in universities. Thus, by 1980, the percentages of students of the relevant age group would be 96·0 per cent in high schools, 15·0 per cent in junior colleges, and 32·0 per cent in universities. The increased enrolment in compulsory education would be due to the natural increase of children in that age group, and no change in the attendance rate of 99·8 per cent was foreseen. The cost of expansion of these enrolments, i.e. the corresponding teaching and administrative forces, and buildings and equipment, was estimated at a total of 56 million yen between 1971 and 1980. The annual cost would increase from 3 billion yen in 1971 to 9·4 billion yen in 1980, but the percentage of this cost in the national income would decrease in these years from 4·6 to 4·5 per cent due to the estimated increase in the national income.

In addition, the Council calculated the cost of kindergartens, special education, pilot projects for the new school ladders, and in-service postgraduate training of teachers in ten years at a total of 5·7 billion yen. Among the above items, the pilot projects were to start in 1974 and the in-service training in 1975.

The Council further projected the improvements in ten years in such items as teachers' salaries, class sizes in elementary and secondary schools, private universities, and graduate school education. The cost was estimated at a total of 10·3 billion yen. Among the above items, the improvement in private universities was aimed at bringing up their faculty—student ratio and educational cost per student to a level of 50 per cent — the same as that in universities. The graduate programmes were to be expanded in enrolment from 6·7 per cent of the university graduates in 1970 to 15·2 per cent in 1980.

In total, the Council estimated the cost for national education between 1971 and 1980 at some 72 billion yen. The annual cost would increase from 3 billion yen to 13 billion in these ten years, and its percentage of the national income would also increase from 4·9 to 6·3 per cent in the same period. The distribution of the above 72 billion yen among the different levels of education would be 4·6 per cent for pre-school education, 53·7 per cent for compulsory, 16·1 per cent for high school, and 25·6 per cent for higher education. In 1971 the State paid 1 billion yen out of 3 billion, and the rest was paid by the local authorities, 1·2 billion yen by the prefectures, and 0·8 billion by municipalities. The Council did not make any mention of the distribution of the 13 billion yen in 1980.

These estimates, though appearing enormous, seemed in fact to be still conservative in view of the real needs. The Council admitted that the expansion would require a large increase in the teaching force, some 35 per cent increase in elementary and secondary teachers within ten years, and included in its estimates was the cost for the expansion of teacher training. In the case of higher education the Council calculated the demand of additional teaching personnel in 1980 at 16,000, out of which, however, only 8500 would be supplied from the graduate schools. The remaining 7500 were expected to be filled by those matured individuals who would turn to teaching from other professions. These expectations seemed to be too optimistic, and there would be a great shortage unless graduate programmes were further expanded.

This indicates the necessity of further investment in higher education, which was pointed out among other things by the OECD examiners. They noted that, while the total investment in education in Japan was quite comparable to that of the other major OECD nations (roughly 7 per cent of the GNP), investment in higher education was notably less. They also pointed out Japan's under-investment in basic and applied research, particularly by the government.

These facts were naturally known to the Japanese. The Ministry of Education itself in its White Paper of 1970 had mentioned that both the percentage of public school education expenditure allocated to higher education and that of national income allocated to higher education had risen rapidly in recent years in all major countries except in Japan, where that had continued to be rather stagnant.

Table 13 indicates the percentage of public school education expenditure allocated to higher education and the percentage of national income allocated to higher education in Japan, the United States, England and Wales, and the Federal Republic of Germany.

The Prime Minister's Council on Science and Technology in its report, *Policies for Science and Technology in the 1970s,* published in April 1971, also pointed out the shortage of investment in research. It recommended that the investment should be increased up to the level of 3 per cent of the

Table 13

	Percentage of public school education expenditure allocated to higher education	Percentage of national income allocated to higher education
Japan		
1962	14·9	0·6
1968	15·7	0·7
United States		
1963	23·9	1·4
1968	27·6	1·9
England and Wales		
1963	17·6	0·6
1967	22·9	1·0
Federal Republic of Germany		
1961	18·3	0·9
1966	24·6	1·1

Quoted from Ministry of Education Japan, *Educational Standards in Japan*, 1970, pp. 145–6.

national income from the present one of 1·9 per cent, and that the proportion of government investment in basic and applied research should be raised from the present rate of 30 per cent of the total made by both public and private sources to over 50 per cent, the rate which the other advanced countries presently observed. Thus, the under-financing in Japanese higher education was evident. As the OECD examiners expressed it, this might have been appropriate in the past when Japan was mainly concerned with borrowing science and technology from the advanced nations, but at this stage, when it stood in the forefront of the world in industry and science, its further progress would depend very much on its own efforts in higher education and learning. A drastic change in policy to break the stagnation in investment on higher education would be one of the keys of Japan's progress in the 1970s.

JAPANESE EDUCATION FOR THE WORLD COMMUNITY

The OECD examiners in their report made special mention of Japanese education in view of Japan's increased participation in the world community. They commented on the closed nature of Japanese national education, and suggested the improvement of the teaching of foreign languages in schools and encouragement of Japanese young people to study abroad, the opening up of Japanese schools and universities to foreigners as both teachers and students, and the training of manpower for world needs. They also suggested the necessity for a change in the basic attitudes of the Japanese, from seeing the world as a market for resources and products to seeing the world as a stage for international co-operation.

The JTU's report also spared one chapter for international solidarity in education. It criticized the government's efforts on international co-operation in education as part of the latter's attempt to become a "great nation" in the political, economic, and military sense. It suggested that education for international solidarity of the nations should be carried out through the teaching of peace and human rights and through the histories of different peoples. It further suggested the revision of school curricula on the above lines, the improvement of international exchanges of students and teachers, assistance in the education of the Korean residents in Japan, the exchange with teachers' unions abroad, and the improvement of the teaching of foreign languages.

Making a sharp contrast to these two contemporary reports of the OECD and the JTU, the 1971 report of the Central Council made very few remarks on education for the world community. This is somewhat puzzling, as the Central Council had already touched on this problem in its report on the "Image of the Ideal Japanese" in 1966, giving consideration to the new qualities of the Japanese in the international community. It may also be pointed out that the international aspects were not lacking in Japanese education; education for international understanding has been one of the important features in Japanese schools since Japan's admission to Unesco in 1951, and educational and cultural exchanges have been expanded year by year. In the 1960s the government began to exert its efforts for educational assistance to the developing nations, and expected to expand it further in the 1970s.

As it turned out, however, the Central Council did not give any serious thought to education for international co-operation or for the world community in its 1971 report, and the problem was handed over to the next Central Council, the members of which were newly appointed by the Minister of Education in May 1972, and were asked by him to consider "international exchanges in education, higher learning and culture". Their report was expected to appear in two years.*

Although it is certainly premature to judge the deliberations of the new council, the terms of reference given by the Minister suggest the limitation of the government's thinking on this issue. As the reports of the OECD and JTU indicated, international exchange, though important, is only one aspect of the broader issue which now in the early 1970s is facing Japan. The problem is: what should national education be like if Japan is to co-operate with other nations in a world community which is becoming so small and so interdependent? As the OECD report stated, Japan should not, and cannot, any longer consider the world "a market of resources in which skills and raw materials could be acquired and products sold". What is expected from Japan is its "international participation on behalf of the world". This change in basic attitudes will require a certain organized effort, for which the national education of Japan must be responsible.

It can be said without fear of over-exaggeration that Japanese national education has successfully instilled the people with a sense of national purpose in time of peace and war. Whether this same national education can be equally effective in producing people for a world community is certainly a big question so long as the existing Japanese schools, universities, and other educational institutions remain unchanged in their orientation. The reorientation of national education, however, will be no easy task.

For one thing, it will require a radical self-examination of Japanese traditions of national education. At the end of World War II there was a chance for this to take place, but, as has been already observed, the general trend in the early 1970s in Japan is, despite certain efforts in the opposite

*In May 1974 the Central Council for Education submitted to the Minister of Education its report "On the International Exchange in Education, Science, and Culture". The report described the objectives of the international exchange as (1) to educate the Japanese people for international responsibility, (2) to deepen the understanding of foreigners of Japan and of the Japanese people of other nations, (3) to develop education, science, and culture through mutual understanding and stimulation, and (4) to participate in international undertaking for the solution of the problems common to human race. In order to achieve these objectives, various measures were suggested in each of the fields of education, science, and culture. In education the report recommended that the improvement should be made especially in the following areas; education for international understanding, teaching of foreign languages, and the exchange of students, teachers, and youths.

direction, faithful to the past, an attitude which has been strengthened by the resurgence of Japan as a powerful nation in economics and technology in the 1960s. As it happened, however, toward the beginning of the new decade, this power in economics and technology became a source of trouble for Japan, both on the domestic and international fronts, as can be seen in the environmental crisis by pollution and the international trade and monetary tension.

It is true that national traditions are important, and that many educational reforms introduced after World War II against the Japanese traditions were eventually modified or abolished. On the other hand, one should be aware that such national traditions in education were nourished and developed under the particular national conditions of Japan. Among its principal features, mention should be made, especially in relation to the question of education for the world community, of the fact that Japan is almost the only nation in the world whose population — exceeding over 100 million — still consists of a single national group with a common historical heritage, a single language, and relative homogeneity in culture and belief. There is no doubt that such unity contributed to the swift modernization of Japan and assisted during this process in creating certain features of its national tradition in education, such as the centralization of control and uniformity in the content of education.

It should be noted, however, that such unity of national composition, which worked positively in the past age of nationalism, would have a bad effect in an age of the world community, where multiplicity of race, tradition, language, culture, and belief is characteristic. Many of the difficulties that the Japanese people are finding in the present international community, both on national and individual levels, can be attributed to their inexperience in this multiplicity. As Japan's international activities expand, such difficulties will increase further unless this handicap is overcome by some organized effort, among which education is of prime importance. To be effective in the new task, however, the national education must first overcome some of the traditions which have developed in the past closely related to the mono-racial composition of the Japanese.

As the above example indicated, the necessity of reorienting the national education is evident. Whether Japan succeeds in this reorientation has still to be seen. This is, however, not a matter or choice, but of national survival. The author, for one, trusts that the Japanese will successfully readjust their national education to an age of the world community.

References*

Anderson, R. S., *Japan: Three Epochs of Modern Education*, U.S. Department of Health, Education, and Welfare, Office of Education, Washington D.C., 1959.

Aso, M. and Amano, I., *Education and Japan's Modernization*, Ministry of Foreign Affairs, Tokyo, Japan, 1972.

Bureau of Statistics, Office of the Prime Minister, Japan, *Statistical Handbook of Japan*, Tokyo, issued annually.

Blewett, J. E. (edit. and trans.), *Higher Education in Postwar Japan – The Ministry of Education's 1964 White Paper*, Sophia University Press, Tokyo, 1955.

Duke, B. C., *Japan's Militant Teachers, A History of the Left-wing Teachers' Movement*, The University Press of Hawaii, Honolulu, 1973.

Japanese National Commission for Unesco, *The Role of Education in the Social and Economic Development of Japan*, Institute for Democratic Education, Tokyo, 1966.

Kaigo, T., *Japanese Education – Its Past and Present*, Kokusai Bunka Shinkokai, Tokyo, 1968.

Ministry of Education, Japan, *Japan's Growth and Education*, Tokyo, 1963.

Ministry of Education, Japan, *Education in Japan – A Graphic Presentation*, Tokyo, 1971.

Ministry of Education, Japan, *Educational Standards in Japan – The 1970 White Paper on Education*, Tokyo, 1971.

Ministry of Education, Japan, *Basic Guidelines for the Reform of Education – Report of the Central Council for Education*, Tokyo, 1972.

Nagai, M., *Higher Education in Japan: Its Take-off and crash*, University of Tokyo Press, Tokyo, 1971.

OECD, *Japan – Reviews of National Policies for Education*, Organization for Economic Co-operation and Development, Paris, 1971.

Passin, H., *Society and Education in Japan*, Bureau of Publications, Teachers College and East Asian Institute, Columbia University, New York, 1965.

Teichler, U. and Voss, F., *Bibliography on Japanese Education: Postwar Publications in Western Languages*, Verlag Documentation, Pullach bei München, 1974.

*English publications only.

Appendix

Chart 1. Organization of school system in 1974

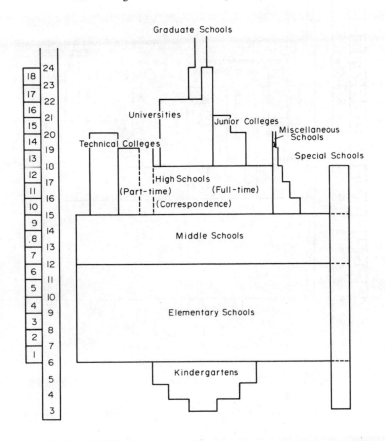

Chart II. Organization of school system around 1940

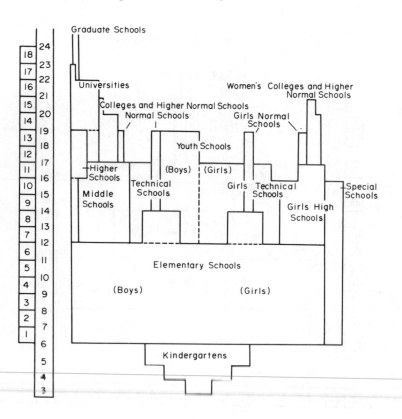

Chart III. Historical trends in Enrolment

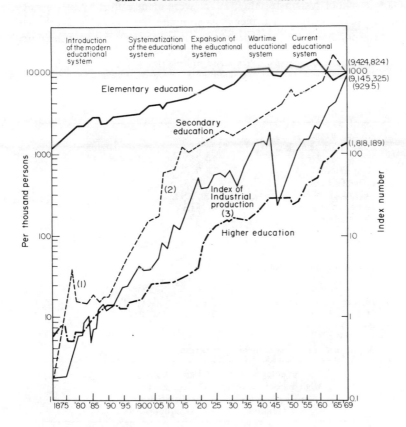

Notes: (1) By the Education Order of 1878, some sub-standard schools were excluded from the number of regular secondary schools.
(2) Pupils in upper elementary schools were counted as secondary school enrollment.
(3) 1935 = 100.
Quoted from Ministry of Education, Japan, *Education in Japan – a Graphic Presentation,* 1971, p.17.

Note on the statistics for 1975

In the last stage of the preparation of this book some statistics on Japanese school system for May, 1975, were made public by the Japanese Ministry of Education. A reader may compare the following figures with the corresponding ones for earlier years quoted in the preceding chapters.

1. Number of schools, colleges and universities, and of their pupils and students

	Number of Institutions	Number of Students (in thousands)
Kindergartens	13,108	2,292
Elementary schools	24,652	10,365
Middle schools	10,751	4,762
High schools	4,946	4,333
Special schools	578	64
Technical colleges	65	48
Junior colleges	513	354
Universities	420	1,734
Miscellaneous schools	7,996	1,212

2. The enrolment rates

Kindergartens	63.5%	
Elementary schools	99.89%	(1974)
Middle schools	99.90%	(1974)

3. The rates of access to higher institutions

	Percentages of High School Entrants to Middle School Graduates	Percentages of College Entrants to High School Graduates
Total	91.9	34.7
Male	91.0	33.8
Female	93.0	34.6

Index